Power

OVER
SATAN

Power

OVER
SATAN

CHARLES Spurgeon

🔲 Whitaker House

All Scripture quotations are taken from the *King James Version* of the Holy Bible.

POWER OVER SATAN
(Previously entitled *Satan, a Defeated Foe*)

ISBN: 0-88368-595-7
Printed in the United States of America
Copyright © 1997 by Whitaker House

Whitaker House
30 Hunt Valley Circle
New Kensington, PA 15068

Library of Congress Cataloging in Publication Data

Spurgeon, C. H. (Charles Haddon). 1834–1892.
    [Satan, a defeated foe]
    Power over Satan / by Charles Spurgeon
       p. cm.
    Originally published: Satan, a defeated foe. Springdale, PA:
Whitaker House, 1993.
    ISBN 0-88368-595-7 (pbk.)
    1. Devil. 2. Spiritual warfare. 3. Christian life—Baptist authors.
I. Title.

BT981 S68 2000
235'.47—dc 21   00-020322

1 2 3 4 5 6 7 8 9 10 11 12 13 14 / 10 09 08 07 06 05 04 03 02 01 00

Contents

One

Satan Considers
the Saints

And the LORD said unto Satan,
Hast thou considered my servant Job?
—Job 1:8

How very uncertain are all terrestrial
things! How foolish are those believers
who lay up their treasure anywhere
except in heaven! Job's prosperity promised
about as much stability as anything beneath the moon can. Undoubtedly, the man
had around him a large household of devoted
and attached servants. He had accumulated

wealth of a kind that does not suddenly depreciate in value. He had oxen, donkeys, and cattle. He did not have go to markets or fairs and trade with his goods to procure food and clothing. He carried on the processes of agriculture on a very large scale around his own homestead and probably grew within his own estate everything that his establishment required. His children were numerous enough to promise a long line of descendants. His prosperity needed nothing to make it complete. It had come to its flood tide; what could make it ebb?

Up there, beyond the clouds, where no human eye could see, there was a scene enacted that heralded no good for Job's prosperity. The spirit of evil stood face to face with the infinite Spirit of all good. An extraordinary conversation took place between these two beings.

When called to account for his doings, the Evil One boasted that he had gone *"to and fro in the earth, and* [walked] *up and down on it"* (Job 1:7), insinuating that he had met with no hindrance to his will and that he had found no one to oppose his moving freely and acting at his own pleasure. He had marched everywhere like a king in his own dominions, unhindered and unchallenged.

The great God reminded Satan that there was at least one place among men where he had no foothold and where his power was unrecognized, namely, in the heart of Job. There was one man who stood like an impregnable castle, garrisoned by integrity and held with perfect loyalty as the possession of the King of heaven.

The Evil One defied God Almighty to try the faithfulness of Job by telling Him that the patriarch's integrity was due to his prosperity, and that he served God and shunned evil from sinister motives because he found his conduct profitable to himself. The God of heaven took up the challenge of the Evil One and gave him permission to take away all the mercies that were supposed to be the props of Job's integrity. God allowed him to pull down all the supports and buttresses and see whether the tower would not stand in its own inherent strength without them. In consequence of this, all Job's wealth went in one black day, and not even a child was left to whisper comfort.

A second interview between the Lord and His fallen angel took place. Job was again the subject of conversation. The Great One, again defied by Satan, permitted him even to touch Job in his bone and in his flesh, until the prince became worse than a pauper. He who was rich and happy was poor and wretched, filled with disease from head to foot and reduced to scraping himself with a broken piece of pottery to gain a poor relief from his pain.

Let us see in this the changeability of all earthly things. *"He hath founded it upon the seas"* (Psalm 24:2) is David's description of this world. Since it is founded on the seas, can you be surprised that it changes often? Do not put your trust in anything underneath the stars. Remember that the word *change* is written on the forefront of nature. Therefore, do not say, "My mountain stands firm; it will never be moved." The glance of the Almighty's eye can shake your mountain into dust; the touch of His foot can make it melt like wax or go up in smoke.

> *If ye then be risen with Christ, seek those things which are above, where Christ sitteth on the right hand of God.*
> *Set your affection on things above, not on things on the earth.*
> (Colossians 3:1–2)

Let your heart and your treasure be *"where neither moth nor rust doth corrupt, and where thieves do not break through nor steal"* (Matthew 6:20).

The words of Bernard may help to instruct us:

> That is the true and chief joy which is not conceived from the creature, but received from the Creator, which (being once possessed thereof) none can take from thee: compared with which all other pleasure is torment, all joy is grief, sweet things are bitter, all glory is baseness, and all delectable things are despicable.

This is not, however, our subject in this chapter. Accept what I have written as merely an introduction to our main discussion. The Lord asked Satan, *"Hast thou considered my servant Job?"* Let us deliberate, first, in what sense the Evil One may be said to consider the people of God. Then, let us notice what it is that he considers about them. Finally, let us comfort ourselves by the reflection that One who is far above Satan considers us in a higher sense.

Satan's Considerations

First, then, in what sense may Satan be said to *"consider"* the people of God? Certainly not in the usual biblical meaning of the term *consider*, as in these verses: *"O*

LORD; *consider my trouble"* (Psalm 9:13), or
"Consider my meditation" (Psalm 5:1), or
"Blessed is he that considers the poor"
(Psalm 41:1). Such consideration implies
goodwill and a careful inspection of the object of benevolence with regard to a wise
distribution of favor.

In that sense, Satan never considers
anyone. If he has any benevolence, it must
be toward himself. All his considerations of
other creatures are of the most malevolent
kind. No meteoric flash of good flits across
the black midnight of his soul, nor does he
consider us as we are told to consider the
works of God, that is, in order to derive instruction as to God's wisdom and love and
kindness. He does not honor God by what
he sees in His works or in His people. It is
not in him to *"go to the ant, thou sluggard;
consider her ways, and be wise"* (Proverbs
6:6). Rather, he goes to the Christian and
considers his ways and becomes more foolishly God's enemy than he was before.

The consideration that Satan pays to
God's saints is this: he regards them with
wonder when he considers the difference
between them and himself. A traitor, when
he knows the thorough villainy and black-
ness of his own heart, cannot help being
astounded when he is forced to believe that

another man is faithful. The first resort of a treacherous heart is to believe that all men would be just as treacherous, and are really so at bottom. The traitor thinks that all men are traitors like himself, or would be, if it paid them better than fidelity.

When Satan looks at the Christian and finds him faithful to God and to His truth, he considers him as we consider a phenomenon—perhaps despising him for his folly, yet marveling at him and wondering how he can act this way. He seems to say, "I, a prince, a peer of God's parliament, would not submit my will to the Almighty. I thought it better to reign in hell than serve in heaven. I did not keep my proper domain, but fell from my throne. How is it that these stand? What grace is it that keeps these? I was a vessel of gold, and yet I was broken. These are earthen vessels, but I cannot break them! I could not stand in my glory—what can be the matchless grace that upholds them in their poverty, in their obscurity, in their persecution, still faithful to the God who does not bless and exalt them as He did me!"

It may be that he also wonders at their happiness. He feels within himself a seething sea of misery. There is an unfathomable gulf of anguish within his soul. When he looks at believers, he sees them quiet in their souls, full of peace and happiness, often without any outward means by which they are comforted, yet rejoicing and full of glory.

Satan goes up and down through the world and possesses great power. There are many slaves to serve him, yet he does not have the happiness of spirit possessed by yonder humble working woman, obscure, unknown, stretched out on the bed of weakness, having no servants to wait on her. He admires and hates the peace that reigns in the believer's soul.

His consideration may go further than this. Do you not think that he considers them to detect, if possible, any flaw and fault in them, by way of solace to himself? "They are not pure," says he, "these blood-bought ones, these elect from before the foundation of the world. They still sin! These adopted children of God, for whom the glorious Son bowed His head and breathed His last, even they offend!"

How he must chuckle, with such delight as he is capable of, over the secret sins of God's people. If he can see anything in them inconsistent with their profession, anything that appears to be deceitful and thus like himself, he rejoices. Each sin born in the believer's heart cries to him, "My father! My father!" Then he feels something like the joy of fatherhood as he sees his foul offspring. He looks at the *"old man"* (Ephesians 4:22) in the Christian and admires the tenacity with which it maintains its hold, the force and vehemence with which it struggles for mastery. He gleefully observes the craft and cunning with which every now and then, at set intervals, at convenient opportunities, the old nature puts forth all its force. He considers our sinful flesh and makes it one of the books in which he diligently reads.

One of the fairest prospects the Devil's eye ever rests on is the inconsistency and the impurity that he can discover in the true child of God. In this respect, he had very little to consider in God's true servant, Job.

This is just the starting point of his consideration. I do not doubt that he views the Lord's people, and especially the more prominent leaders among them, as the great barriers to the progress of his kingdom. Just as the engineer, endeavoring to make a railway, keeps his eye very much fixed on the hills and rivers, and especially on the great mountain through which it will take months to laboriously bore a tunnel, so Satan, in looking upon his various plans to carry on his dominion in the world, considers men like Job.

Satan must have thought much about Martin Luther. "I could ride the world over," he probably said, "if it were not for that monk. He stands in my way. That strong-headed man hates and attacks my kingdom. If I could get rid of him, I would not mind if fifty thousand smaller saints stood in my way."

He is sure to consider God's servant if there is *"none like him"* (Job 1:8), if he stands out distinct and separate from others. Those of us who are called to the work of the ministry must expect from our position to be selected as the special objects of his consideration. When the magnifying glass is at the eye of that dreadful warrior, he is sure to look out for those who by their uniforms are discovered to be the officers, and he tells his sharpshooters to be very careful to aim at these. "For," he says, "if the standard-bearer falls, then the victory will be more readily gained for our side, and our opponents will be easily put to flight."

If you are more generous than other believers, if you live nearer to God than others, as the birds peck most at the ripest fruit, so may you expect Satan to be most busy against you. Who cares to contend for a province covered with stones and barren rocks, and ice-bound by frozen seas? But in all times there sure to be a contention after the fertile valleys where the crops are plenteous and where the farmer's toil is well rewarded. Thus, for you who honor God most, Satan will struggle very sternly. He wants to pluck God's jewels from His crown, if he can, and take the Redeemer's precious stones even from the breastplate itself.

In this way, Satan considers God's people. Viewing them as hindrances to his reign, he contrives methods by which he may remove them out of his way or turn them to his own account. Darkness would cover the earth if he could blow out the lights. There would be no fruit to wave like the cedars of Lebanon if he could destroy that handful of corn upon the top of the mountains (Psalm 72:16). Hence, his perpetual consideration is to make the faithful fall from among men.

It does not require much wisdom to discern that the great object of Satan in considering God's people is to do them injury. I scarcely think he hopes to destroy the really chosen and blood-bought heirs of life. My notion is that he is too smart for that.

He has been foiled so often when he has attacked God's people that he can hardly think he will be able to destroy the elect.

You remember what the soothsayers, who are very closely related to him, said to Haman: *"If Mordecai be of the seed of the Jews, before whom thou hast begun to fall, thou shalt not prevail against him, but shalt surely fall before him."* (Esther 6:13). He knows very well that there is a royal seed in the land against whom he fights in vain.

It strikes me that if he could be absolutely certain that any one soul was chosen by God, he would scarcely waste his time in attempting to destroy it, although he might seek to worry and to dishonor it. However, most likely Satan no more knows who God's elect are than we do, for he can only judge as we do, by outward actions, even though he can form a more accurate judgment than we can, by reason of his longer experience and his ability to see persons in private where we cannot intrude. Yet into God's book of secret decrees, his black eye can never peer. *"By their fruits"* (Matthew 7:16) he knows them, and we know them in the same manner.

Since, however, we are often mistaken in our judgment, he, too, may be also. And it seems to me that he therefore makes it his policy to endeavor to destroy us all—not knowing in which case he may succeed. He goes about *"seeking whom he may devour"* (1 Peter 5:8), and since he does not know whom he may be permitted to swallow up, he attacks all the people of God with vehemence.

Someone may ask, "How can one devil do this?" He does not do it by himself. I do not know that many of us have ever been tempted directly by Satan—we may not be notable enough among men to be worth his trouble. But he has a whole host of inferior spirits under his supremacy and control. As the centurion said of himself, so he might have also said of Satan, "[He says to this spirit], *Go, and he goeth; and to another, Come, and he cometh; and to my servant, Do this, and he doeth it"* (Matthew 8:9). Thus all the servants of God will more or less come under the direct or indirect assaults of the Great Enemy of souls, and these attacks are with the aim of destroying them. For he would, *"if it were possible...deceive the very elect"* (Matthew 24:24).

In situations where he cannot destroy, there is no doubt that Satan's object is to worry and to bother. He does not like to see God's people happy. I believe the Devil greatly delights in some ministers, whose tendency in their preaching is to multiply and foster doubts and fears and to present grief and despondency as the primary evidences of being one of God's family. "Oh, yes," says the Devil, "preach on. You are doing my work well, for I like to see God's people mournful. If I can make them stop their singing and go around with miserable faces, I reckon I have done my work very completely."

My dear friends, let us watch against those deceptive temptations that pretend to make us humble but really aim at making us unbelieving. Our God takes no delight in our suspicions and mistrusting. See how He proves His love in the gift of His dear Son Jesus. Banish, then, all your doubts and worries, and rejoice in unshakeable confidence. God delights to be worshipped with joy.

> *Oh come, let us sing to the LORD! Let us shout joyfully to the Rock of our salvation.*
> *Let us come before His presence with thanksgiving; Let us shout joyfully to Him with psalms.* (Psalm 95:1–2)
>
> *Be glad in the LORD and rejoice, you righteous; and shout for joy, all you upright in heart!* (Psalm 32:11)

Rejoice in the Lord always. Again I will say, rejoice! (Philippians 4:4)

Satan resents hearing God praised by His children. Martin Luther used to say, "Let us sing psalms and spite the Devil." I have no doubt Martin Luther was pretty nearly right, for that lover of discord hates harmonious, joyous praise.

Beloved friend, the Archenemy wants to make you wretched here if he cannot have you hereafter. In this, no doubt, he is aiming a blow at the honor of God. He is well aware that mournful Christians often dishonor the faithfulness of God by mistrusting it. Thus he thinks if he can worry us until we no longer believe in the constancy and goodness of the Lord, he will have robbed God of His praise. *"Whoso offereth praise, glorifieth Me"* (Psalm 50:23), says God. So Satan swings the ax at the root of our praise so that God may cease to be glorified.

Moreover, if Satan cannot destroy a Christian, how often has he spoiled his usefulness? Many believers have fallen, not so as to break their necks and die prematurely—that is impossible—but they have broken some important bone and have gone limping to their graves! We can recall with grief some men who were once prominent in the church and who were running well, but who suddenly through the stress of temptation fell into sin. Their names were never mentioned in the church again except with bated breath. Everybody thought and prayed that they were saved *"as through fire"* (1 Corinthians 3:15), but certainly their former usefulness could hardly return. It is very easy to go backwards in the heavenly pilgrimage, but it is very difficult to retrieve your steps.

You may turn aside and blow out your candle, but you cannot light it again quite as quickly. Beloved in the Lord, watch against the attacks of Satan and stand fast, because you, as a pillar in the house of God, are very dear to the church. We cannot spare you. As a father or as a mother in our midst, we honor you, and we do not wish to mourn and lament or to be grieved by hearing the shouts of our adversaries while they cry, "Aha! This is just what we wanted!"

Alas, there have been many things done in our midst about which we say: *"Tell it not in Gath, publish it not in the streets of Askelon; lest the daughters of the Philistines rejoice, lest the daughters of the uncircumcised triumph"* (2 Samuel 1:20).

May God grant us grace as a church to stand against the schemes of Satan and his attacks, that having done his worst, he may gain no advantage over us. After having considered, reconsidered, and carefully counted our towers and bulwarks, may he be compelled to retire because his battering rams cannot jar so much as a stone from our ramparts, and his slings cannot slay one single soldier on the walls.

Before I leave this point, I would like to address a question that is often asked, if only in the minds of believers: "Why is it that God permits this constant and malevolent consideration of His people by the Evil One?"

Undoubtedly, one answer is that God knows what is for His own glory, and that He gives no account of His matters. Having permitted free agency and having allowed for some mysterious reason the existence of evil, it does not seem agreeable with His having done so to destroy Satan. Rather, He allows the fiend to have power so that it may be a fair hand-to-hand fight between sin and holiness, between grace and craftiness.

Incidentally, let it also be remembered that the temptations of Satan are of service to the people of God. Fénelon said that they serve as the file that rubs off much of the rust of self-confidence. I may add that they make a horrible sound in the sentinel's ear, which is sure to keep him awake. One astute theologian remarked that there is no temptation in the world as bad as not being tempted at all, for to be tempted will tend to keep us awake. On the other hand, flesh and blood become weak and anemic without temptation. Though our spirits may be willing, yet we may be found falling into slumber. (See Matthew 26:40–41.)

Children do not run away from their father's side when big dogs bark at them. The howling of the Devil may tend to drive us nearer to Christ, may teach us our own weaknesses, may keep us upon our own watchtower, and may be made the means of preservation from other ills. *"Be sober, be vigilant; because your adversary the devil, as a roaring lion, walketh about, seeking whom he may devour"* (1 Peter 5:8).

May we who are in a prominent position be permitted to affectionately make one earnest request of you: *"Brethren, pray for us"* (1 Thessalonians 5:25), that exposed as we are to the consideration of Satan, we may be guarded by divine power. Let us be made rich by your faithful prayers so that we may be kept even to the end.

Satan's Injurious Viewpoint

Now then, specifically what does Satan consider with the view toward the injury of God's people?

It cannot be said of him, as it is of God, that he knows us totally. However, since he has now been dealing with poor fallen humanity for six thousand years or so, he must have acquired very vast experience in that period of time. Having been all over the earth and having tempted the highest and the lowest, he must know very well what the springs of human action are and how to play upon them.

Satan watches and considers, first of all, our particular infirmities and weak points where we are vulnerable. The Enemy of our souls soon finds out where we are faulty when he looks us up and down, just as I have seen a horse dealer do with a horse. I, a common observer, might think a horse an exceedingly good one as I see it running up and down the road, but the dealer sees what I cannot see and knows how to handle the creature in such a way that he soon discovers any hidden mischief. Satan knows how to look at us and size us up from heel to head, so that he says of this man, "His infirmity is lust"; of that one, "He has a quick temper"; of another, "He is proud"; or of that other, "He is slothful."

His eye of malice is very quick to perceive a weakness, and the hand of enmity soon takes advantage of it. When the Archenemy finds a weak place in the walls of our castles, he takes care where to plant his battering ram and begin his siege. You may conceal your infirmity even from your dearest friend, but you will not conceal it from your worst Enemy. He has lynx eyes and detects in a moment the weak point in your armor. He goes about with a match, and though you may think you have covered all the gunpowder of your heart, he knows how to find a crack to put his match through. Much mischief will he do unless eternal mercy prevents.

He takes care also to consider our state of mind. If the Devil would attack us when our minds are in certain moods, we would be more than a match for him. He knows this and shuns the encounter. Some men are more vulnerable to temptation when they are distressed and desponding. The Fiend will then assail them. Others will be more liable to catch fire when they are jubilant and full of joy, so that is when he will strike his spark into the tinder. Certain people, when they are overly vexed and tossed to and fro, can be made to say almost anything. Others, when their souls are like perfectly placid waters, are just then in a condition to be navigated by the Devil's vessel.

As a metalworker knows that one metal is to be worked with at a particular heat and another at a different temperature, and as those who have to deal with chemicals know that at a certain heat one fluid will boil while another reaches the boiling point much earlier, so Satan knows exactly the temperature at which to work on us for his purpose. Small pots boil quickly when they are put on the fire, and so do little men with quick tempers. Larger vessels require more time and heat before they will boil, but when they do, it is a boil indeed, not soon forgotten or abated.

The Enemy, like a veteran fisherman, watches his fish, adapts his bait to his prey, and knows in what seasons and times the fish are most likely to bite. This hunter of souls comes secretly. Often we are overtaken in a fault or caught in a trap through an unwatchful frame of mind. That rare collector of choice sayings, Thomas Spencer, said the following, which is much to the point:

The chameleon, when he lies on the grass to catch flies and grasshoppers, takes upon him the color of the grass, as the polypus does the color of the rock under which he lurks, that the fish may boldly come near him without any suspicion of danger. In like manner, Satan turns himself into that shape that we least fear, and sets before us such objects of temptation as are most agreeable to our natures, so he may the sooner draw us into his net; he sails with every wind, and blows us the way that we incline ourselves through the weakness of nature.

Is our knowledge in the matter of faith deficient? He tempts us to error. Is our conscience tender? He tempts us to scrupulosity, and too much preciseness. Has our conscience, like the ecliptic line, some latitude? He tempts us to carnal liberty. Are we bold-spirited? He tempts us to presumption. Are we timorous and distrustful? He tempts us to desperation. Are we of a flexible disposition? He tempts us to inconstancy. Are we stiff? He labors to make obstinate heretics, schismatics, or rebels of us. Are we of an austere temper? He tempts us to cruelty. Are we soft and mild? He tempts us to indulgence and foolish pity. Are we hot in matters of religion? He tempts us to blind zeal and superstition. Are we cold? He tempts us to Laodicean lukewarmness. Thus he lays his traps, that one way or other, he may ensnare us.

Satan also takes care to consider our position among men. There are a few people who are most easily tempted when they are alone. They are then subjected to great heaviness of mind, and they may be driven to most awful crimes. Perhaps most of us are more liable to sin when we are in the company of others. In some company I would never be led into sin, but I could scarcely venture into other groups. Many are so full of levity that those of us who are inclined the same way can scarcely look them in the face without feeling our own besetting sin rising. Others are so somber that if they meet a brother of a similar mind, they are pretty sure between them to invent an evil report of the good land. Satan knows where to overtake you in a place where you lie open to his attacks. He will pounce upon you, swooping like a bird of prey from the sky, where he has been watching for the moment to make his descent with the prospect of success.

How, too, he considers our condition in the world! He looks at one man and says,

"That man has property; it is of no use my trying these certain deceits with him. But here is another man who is very poor; I will catch him in that net." Then, again, he looks at the poor man and says, "Now, I cannot tempt him to this folly, but I will lead the rich man into it." As the sportsman has one gun for wild fowl and another for deer and game, so Satan has a different temptation for various orders of men. I do not suppose that the Queen's temptation ever will annoy the housekeeper. I do not suppose, on the other hand, that the housekeeper's temptation will ever be very serious to me. Probably you could escape from mine, though I do not think you could. I sometimes imagine I could bear yours, though I question if I could. Satan knows, however, just where to smite each of us. Our position, our capabilities, our education, our standing in society, our calling—all may be doors through which he may attack us.

You who have no calling at all are in special peril. I wonder that the Devil does not swallow you instantly. The most likely man to go to hell is the man who has nothing to do on earth. I say that seriously. I believe that a much worse evil cannot happen to a person than to be placed where he has no work. If I should ever be in such a state, I would get employment at once for fear I would be carried off, body and soul, by the Evil One. Idle people tempt the Devil to tempt them.

Let us have something to do; let us keep our minds occupied. If we do not, we will make room for the Devil. Industry will not make us gracious, but the lack of work may make us vicious. Always have some work to do. As Isaac Watts penned,

> In books, or work, or healthful play,
> I would be busy too,
> For Satan finds some mischief still
> For idle hands to do.

Books, work, or such recreations as are necessary for health should occupy our time. If I throw myself down in idleness, like an old piece of iron, I must not wonder that I grow rusty with sin.

I am not finished with this subject yet. Satan, when he makes his investigations, notices all the objects of our affection. I do not doubt that when he went around Job's house, he observed it as carefully as thieves do a jeweler's premises when they are planning to break in. They very cunningly take account of every door, window, and lock.

They do not fail to look at the house next door, for they may have to reach the treasure through the building that adjoins it.

When the Devil looked around, jotting down in his mind all Job's position, he thought to himself, "There are the camels, the oxen, the donkeys, and the servants—yes, I can use all these very admirably."

"Then," he thought, "there are the three daughters, there are the seven sons, and they all go feasting. I know where to catch them, and if I can just blow the house down when they are feasting, that will afflict the father's mind more severely, for he will say, 'Oh, that they had died when they had been praying, rather than when they had been feasting and drinking wine.'"

"I will also put his wife down in the inventory," said the Devil, "I dare say I will need her," and accordingly it came to that. Nobody could have done what Job's wife did. None of the servants could have said that sentence so stingingly, or—if she meant it very kindly—none could have said it with such a fascinating air as Job's own wife. "Bless God and die," as it may be read, or usually, *"Curse God, and die"* (Job 2:9). Satan, you have plowed with Job's heifer, but you have not succeeded. Job's strength lies in God, not in his hair, or you might have shaved him just as Samson was shorn!

Perhaps the Evil One had even inspected Job's personal sensitivities, and so selected that form of bodily affliction that he knew to be most dreaded by his victim. He brought upon him a disease that Job may have seen and shuddered at in poor men outside the city gates.

Beloved, Satan knows quite as much in regard to you. You have a child, and Satan knows that you idolize him. "Ah," he says, "there is a place for my wounding him." Even your marriage partner may be made a quiver in which hell's arrows will be stored until the time may come, and then he or she may prove the bow from which Satan will shoot them. Watch your neighbor and your spouse, because you do not know how Satan may try to gain an advantage over you.

Our habits, our joys, our sorrows, our private moments, our public positions—all may be made weapons of attack by this desperate Foe of the Lord's people. We have snares everywhere, in our beds and at our tables, in our houses and in the street. There are snares and traps in company and pits when we are alone. We may find temptations in the house of God as well as in the world, traps in our elevated position, and deadly poisons in our abasement.

We must not expect to be rid of temptations until we have crossed the Jordan, and then, thank God, we are beyond the gunshot of the Enemy. The last howling of the dog of hell will be heard as we descend into the chilly waters of the black stream, but when we hear the hallelujah of the glorified, we will be finished with the Black Prince forever and ever.

Higher Considerations

Satan considered, but there was a higher consideration that overrode his consideration.

In times of war, the military strategists and mine specialists of one side will lay out a minefield. It is a very common counteraction for the other side to undermine the first mines. This is just what God does with Satan. Satan is laying mines, and he plans to light the fuse and blow up God's building. But all the while God is undermining him, and he blows up his own mine before he can do any real mischief.

The Devil is surely the greatest of all fools. He has more knowledge but less wisdom than any other creature. He has more subtlety than all the beasts of the field, but it is well called subtlety, not wisdom. It is not true wisdom; it is only another shape of folly.

All the while that Satan was tempting Job, he little knew that he was answering God's purpose, for God was looking on and considering the whole picture and holding the Enemy as a man holds a horse by its bridle. The Lord had considered exactly how far he would let Satan go.

The first time that Satan came against Job, God did not permit him to touch Job's flesh—perhaps that was more than Job could have borne at that time. Have you ever noticed that if you are in good strong bodily health, you can bear losses and crosses, and even bereavements, with something like calmness? Now that was the case with Job. Perhaps if the disease had come first and the rest had followed, it might have been a temptation too heavy for Job. But God, who knows just how far to let the Enemy go, will say to Satan, "Thus far, and no farther."

By degrees Job became accustomed to his poverty; in fact, the trial had lost all of its sting the moment he said, *"The LORD gave, and the LORD hath taken away"* (Job 1:21). That enemy was slain. It was buried, and this was the funeral oration: *"Blessed be the name of the LORD"* (v. 21).

When the second trial came, the first trial had equipped Job to endure the second. It may be a more severe trial for a man in the possession of great worldly wealth to suddenly be deprived of the bodily power of enjoying it, than to lose everything first and then lose the health necessary for its enjoyment.

Having already lost everything, Job might almost have said, "I thank God that now I have nothing to enjoy, and therefore the loss of the power to enjoy it is not so wearisome. I do not have to say, 'How I wish I could go out in my fields and see to my servants,' because they are all dead. I do not wish to see my children; they are all dead and gone. I am thankful that they are. Better that they are dead than that they should see their poor father sitting on a dunghill like this."

He might have been almost glad if his wife had gone, too, for certainly it was not a particularly merciful blessing when she was spared. Possibly, if he had had all his children around him, it might have been a harder trial than it was. The Lord, who weighs mountains in scales, had meted out his servant's woe.

Did not the Lord also consider how He would sustain his servant under the trial? Beloved, you do not know how blessedly our God poured the secret oil on Job's fire of grace while the Devil was throwing buckets of water on it. He said to Himself, "If Satan does much, I will do more. If he takes away much, I will give more. If he tempts the man to curse, I will fill him so full of love for Me that he will bless Me. I will help him; I will strengthen him; yes, I will uphold him with the right hand of My righteousness." (See Isaiah 41:10.)

Christian, take the following two thoughts and put them under your tongue as a wafer made with honey. You will never be tempted without express license from the throne where Jesus pleads. On the other hand, when He permits it, He *"will with the temptation also make a way of escape"* (1 Corinthians 10:13) or give you grace to stand under it.

In the next place, the Lord considered how to sanctify Job by this trial. Job was a much better man at the end of the story than he was at the beginning. *"That man was perfect* [blameless] *and upright"* (Job 1:1) at first, but there was a little pride about him. We are poor creatures to criticize such a man as Job, but still there was in him a sprinkling of self-righteousness, I think, which his friends brought out. Eliphaz and Zophar said such irritating things that poor Job could not help replying in strong terms about himself, terms that were rather too strong. There was a little too much self-justification in his self-defense.

He was not proud, as some of us are, of a very little. He had much to be proud of, at least in the eyes of the world, but yet there was the tendency to be exalted with it. Though the Devil did not know it, perhaps if he had left Job alone, that pride might have developed fruit, and Job might have sinned. However, he was in such a hurry that he would not let the bad seed ripen, but hastened to destroy it. So the trials became the Lord's tool to bring Job into a more humble and, consequently, a safer and more blessed state of mind.

Moreover, observe how Satan was a lackey to the Almighty! Job all this while was being enabled to earn a greater reward. All his prosperity was not enough. God loved Job so much that He intended to give him twice the property. He intended to give him children again. He meant to make him a more famous man than ever, a man whose name would ring down through the ages, a man who would be talked of through all generations. He was not to be the man of Uz, but of the whole world. He was not to be heard of by a handful in one neighborhood, but all men are to hear of Job's patience in the hour of trial.

Who was to do this? Who was to fashion the trumpet of fame through which Job's name would be blown? The Devil went to the forge and worked away with all his might to make Job illustrious! Foolish Devil! He was piling up a pedestal on which God would set his servant Job, so that he may be looked upon with wonder by all ages.

To conclude, Job's afflictions and Job's patience have been a lasting blessing to the church of God, and they have inflicted incredible disgrace upon Satan. If you want to make the Devil angry, throw the story of Job in his face. If you desire to have your own confidence sustained, may God the Holy Spirit lead you into the patience of Job. How many saints have been comforted in their distress by this story of patience! How many have been saved out of the jaws of the lion and from the paw of the bear by the dark experiences of the patriarch of Uz.

Oh, Archfiend, how you are taken in your own net! You threw a stone that fell on your own head. You made a pit for Job, but fell into it yourself. You are taken in your own craftiness. The Lord God has made fools of the wise and driven the diviners mad.

Beloved, let us commit ourselves in faith to the care and keeping of God. Come poverty, come sickness, come death, we will in all things through Jesus Christ's blood be conquerors. By the power of His Spirit, we will overcome at the last.

I pray that we are all trusting in Jesus. May those who have not trusted Him be led to begin right now. And God will have all the praise in us all, forevermore. Amen.

Two

Satan in a Rage

And there appeared a great wonder in heaven; a woman
clothed with the sun, and the moon under her feet,
and upon her head a crown of twelve stars:
and she being with child cried, travailing in birth,
and pained to be delivered.
And there appeared another wonder in heaven; and
behold a great red dragon, having seven heads
and ten horns, and seven crowns upon his heads.
And his tail drew the third part of the stars of heaven,
and did cast them to the earth: and the dragon stood
before the woman which was ready to be delivered,
for to devour her child as soon as it was born.
And she brought forth a man child,
who was to rule all nations with a rod of iron:

and her child was caught up unto God, and to his throne.
And the woman fled into the wilderness,
where she hath a place prepared of God,
that they should feed her there a thousand
two hundred and threescore days.
And there was war in heaven:
Michael and his angels fought against the dragon;
and the dragon fought and his angels,
and prevailed not; neither was their place found any
more in heaven.
And the great dragon was cast out, that old serpent,
called the Devil, and Satan, which deceiveth
the whole world: he was cast out into the earth,
and his angels were cast out with him.
And I heard a loud voice saying in heaven,
Now is come salvation, and strength,
and the kingdom of our God,
and the power of his Christ:
for the accuser of our brethren is cast down,
which accused them before our God day and night.
And they overcame him by the blood of the Lamb,
and by the word of their testimony;
and they loved not their lives unto the death.
Therefore rejoice, ye heavens,
and ye that dwell in them.

Satan in a Rage

Woe to the inhabiters of the earth and of the sea!
for the devil is come down unto you,
having great wrath, because he knoweth
that he hath but a short time.
And when the dragon saw that he was cast
unto the earth, he persecuted the woman
which brought forth the man child.
And to the woman were given two wings
of a great eagle, that she might fly into the wilderness,
into her place, where she is nourished for a time,
and times, and half a time,
from the face of the serpent.
And the serpent cast out of his mouth
water as a flood after the woman,
that he might cause her to be carried away of the flood.
And the earth helped the woman,
and the earth opened her mouth,
and swallowed up the flood
which the dragon cast out of his mouth.
And the dragon was wroth with the woman,
and went to make war with the remnant of her seed,
which keep the commandments of God,
and have the testimony of Jesus Christ.

—Revelation 12:1–17

The great battle in the heavenlies has been fought. Our glorious Michael has forever overthrown the Dragon and cast him down. In the highest regions, the great principle of evil has received a total defeat through the life and death of our Lord Jesus. Atonement has been made for human sin, and the great quarrel between God and man has come to a happy end. Everlasting righteousness has been brought in, and the peace of God reigns in heaven. The conflict henceforth rages here below. In these inferior regions, the prince of this world is warring mightily against the cause of God and truth. This causes much woe to the sons of men, woe that will never end until Satan's power is totally taken away.

Observe concerning our Archenemy that he exercises forethought and care when he undertakes evil enterprises. Whatever foolish men may do, the Devil is constantly thinking. Others may be heedless and thoughtless, but he is anxious and full of consideration. He knows that his time, or opportunity, is short. He looks ahead to its close, for he is no careless waster of time and forgetter of the end. He values his opportunity to maintain his kingdom, to distress the people of God, and to dishonor the name of Christ. Since he knows it is but a short time, he treats it as such.

He infers the brevity of his time from the victory that Jesus has already gained over him. In reading the twelfth chapter of Revelation, we saw how the Child who is *"to rule all nations with a rod of iron...was caught up unto God, and to his throne"* (v. 5). Then we saw the war in heaven and how the Devil was cast out into the earth and his angels with him. Then a loud voice was heard on high, saying, *"Now is come salvation, and strength, and the kingdom of our God, and the power of his Christ: for the accuser of our brethren is cast down, which accused them before our God day and night"* (v. 10). Very well may the old Serpent conclude that he will be routed on earth since he has already sustained so dire a defeat that he has fallen from heaven, never to rise again. Because the man-child Christ Jesus has met him in conflict, met him when all his power was still unbroken, and has cast him down from his high places, he is persuaded that his reign is ended and that his opportunity is short.

Even now Satan feels a chain around him, which has been lengthened for a while but will be shortened by and by. Then he will roam the earth no longer, but lie as a captive in his prison. Fallen as this apostate spirit has become, he has bright enough wits to look ahead to the future. Oh, that men were half as awake and would remember their end! I beg you to notice this fact concerning the Evil Spirit, that you, too, may learn to acquire knowledge and then use it for practical purposes. Why should it always be that the powers of darkness appear to act more wisely than the children of light? For once I would point out a matter in which our worst Foe may teach us a lesson.

Among men there are some who know a great many important matters but act as if they do not know them. Their knowledge is so much waste heaped up in the storeroom of their minds and never brought into the workshop to be used for practical purposes.

For instance, we know our mortality and yet live as if we were never meant to die. There is great necessity for many of us to pray the following prayer: *"So teach us to number our days, that we may apply our hearts unto wisdom"* (Psalm 90:12). We must know that our time is short and our lives will soon come to an end, yet we fail to know it practically, for we are not as earnest as dying men ought to be. In this the Archenemy is not as foolish as we are, for he knows so well that his time is short that he remembers the fact and is activated by it.

Note well the direction in which this knowledge operates on him. It excites his emotions. The deepest emotion of which he is capable is anger, for he does not know how to love. Wrath is his very soul, as hatred is his very life. He knows nothing of gentleness, nothing of affection, and therefore the fact that his time is short stirs the master passion within him, and he has great wrath. His evil nature is all on fire, and his excitement is terrible.

How much the shortness of our time ought to stir our hearts! With what ardency of love and fervency of zeal ought we to pass the days of our sojourning here! Knowing that the time of our departure is at hand, and that the season in which we can serve God among the sons of men is very brief, we ought to be excited to flaming zeal and passionate love. We are not half as stirred as we ought to be. Devils feel great hatred. Why is it that we do not feel great love? Should they be more eager to destroy than we are to save? Should they be totally alive while we are half dead?

Nor is the result of knowing that his time is short merely emotional on the part of the Archfiend. In consequence of his great wrath, he is moved to make earnest efforts. His energy is excited, he persecutes the woman whose seed he dreads, and he pours a flood of fury out of his mouth against her.

There is nothing that Satan can do for his evil cause that he does not or will not do. We may be halfhearted, but he never is. He is the image of ceaseless industry and untiring earnestness. He will do all that can be done in the range of his permitted time. We may be sure that he will never lose a day.

My beloved, you and I, on the other hand, should be moved by the shortness of our opportunity to an equal energy of incessant industry, serving God continually, because *the night cometh, when no man can work*" (John 9:4). My friend, if you want your children brought to Christ, speak to them, for they will soon be without a father or a mother. If you wish your employees to be saved, labor for their conversion, for they will soon be without an employer. If you desire your brother to be converted, speak to him, for your sisterly love will not help him much longer. Minister, if you want to save your congregation by the Spirit of God, seek to do it at once, for your tongue will soon be silent. Sunday school teacher, if you want your class to be gathered into the Good

Shepherd's fold, treasure every Sunday's opportunities, for soon those who know you now will know you no more forever.

Thus, as of old, *"the Israelites went down to the Philistines, to sharpen every man his [plow]share, and his coulter, and his ax, and his mattock"* (1 Samuel 13:20), so I have urged you to quicken your diligence by the example of the Prince of Darkness. Should we not learn wisdom from his subtlety and zeal from his fury? Will he discern the signs of the times and therefore stir himself, while we sleep on? Will evil encompass the sea and land while the children of God creep about in idleness? God forbid. I entreat you, my friends, awake out of your sleep and see the great wrath of the old Dragon.

In verse twelve, the text tells us that the shortness of Satan's opportunity stirs his wrath. We may put together a general rule from this one statement: in proportion as the Devil's time is shortened, so his energy is increased. We may take it as an assured fact that when he rages to the uttermost, his opportunities are nearly over. He has great wrath, knowing that his time is short. I hope there will be some instruction in this and some comfort for all those who are on the right side. May the Holy Spirit make it so.

In the world around us, we must not think that things are going altogether wrong when the powers of evil become strong. We would be foolish if we wept in despair because the weeds are ripening, for is not the wheat ripening, too? True, the dead become more corrupt, but if the living become more active, why should we lament? Because blasphemy grows thunderous, because infidels seek to undermine the foundation of the faith, or because the clouds of superstition grow ominous, we must not therefore conclude that we have fallen upon evil times, the like of which were never seen before.

Often, the development of evil is an indication that there is an equal or a greater development of good. The high point of ill is frequently its end. Do you not know that in the world of nature the darkest time of night is right before the dawning of the day? Could it not be the same in the spiritual and moral world? Does not the old proverb tell us concerning the year, that "as the day lengthens, the cold strengthens"? As the spring comes with lengthened days, the frosts often grow more sharp and hard. Is it not also plain to the simplest mind that the turning of the tide happens when the ebb has reached its limits?

Just so, when evil is at its height, it is nearest to its fall. Look to the pages of history for confirmation. When no straw was given to make bricks, Moses was used by God to deliver the oppressed. When Pharaoh would by no means let the people go and his yoke seemed riveted upon the neck of Israel, then the right arm of God was made bare (Isaiah 52:10), and the Red Sea beheld His vengeance. When despots grow most tyrannical, liberty's hour is coming. When the lie becomes exceedingly bold and wears a brazen front, then is the time that truth confounds her. When Goliath stalks abroad and defies the armies of Israel, the stone is already in the sling, and David is nearby to lay the giant low.

Do not, therefore, dread the coming of greater opposition or the apparent increase in strength of those oppositions that already exist, for it has always been in the history of events that the hour of the triumph of evil is the hour of its doom. When Belshazzar profanes the holy vessels, the handwriting blazes on the wall. When Haman is at the king's banquet seeking the blood of the whole race of the Jews, the gallows are prepared for him upon his own roof.

Even to the last hour of history, it will be seen that the Devil rages all the more when his empire is nearer to its end. At the very last, he will go about to deceive the nations that are in the four quarters of the earth, Gog and Magog, to gather them together for battle. They will come up in great hosts, brutally fierce for the conflict, to *"the battle of that great day of God Almighty"* (Revelation 16:14) at Armageddon.

At that point, it will seem as if the light of Israel must be quenched and the truth of God utterly extinguished. But in that dread hour, the Lord will triumph gloriously, and He will smite His adversaries in their final overthrow. Then will the angel standing in the sun invite the vultures and all the fowls that fly in the midst of heaven to gather to the grim feast of vengeance, to eat the flesh of horsemen and men of might. Then also will *"the devil who deceived them* [be] *cast into the lake of fire and brimstone...and shall be tormented day and night for ever and ever"* (Revelation 20:10). Then also will be heard the shout, *"Alleluia, for the Lord God omnipotent reigns"* (Revelation 19:6). On the greatest possible scale, the greatness of the Dragon's wrath is a sure prophecy of the end of his reign.

What is true on a great scale is generally true on a small scale. Missionaries in any country will find that the last onslaught of paganism is the most ferocious. We will find that whenever falsehood comes into contact with the truth and error is driven to its last entrenchments, they fight for life, tooth and nail, with all their might. The wrath is great because their time is short. In any village or town in England or in any other country, whenever the opposition to the Gospel reaches its most outrageous pitch and men seem as if they would murder the preacher of the Word, you may reckon that the power of the opposition is almost over.

After the mad fit has run its course, active persecution will cease. There will come a time of calm and, perhaps, of a general reception of the Gospel. Once the bad passions of mankind have boiled up, they will cool down again. Has not God promised to restrain them? As the burning heat of the noon sun does not last forever but gradually abates when it has reached the hottest point, so is it with the wrath of man, which the foul Fiend so often uses for his base purposes.

The same truth will apply to every individual man. When God begins His great work in a sinner's heart to lead him to Christ, it is not a bad sign if the man feels more hatred for God than ever, more dislike for good things than before. We need not despair if he is driven into greater sin than ever. The ferocity of the temptation indicates the vigor with which Satan contends for any of his black sheep. He will not lose his subjects if he can help it, and so he puts forth all his strength to keep them under his power. He is especially diligent and furious when the power of grace is about to prevail for their salvation.

The general fact is further illustrated in the lives of many believers. There are times when, in the believer's heart, the battle rages horribly. That precious child of God hardly knows whether he is a child of God at all and is ready to give up all hope. He cannot pray or praise because he is so distracted. He cannot read the Bible without horrible thoughts. It seems as if he must utterly perish, for no respite is given him in which to refresh his heart, the attacks are so continual and violent. Such dreadful times of attack are often followed by years of peace, quiet usefulness, holiness, and communion with God. Satan knows when God is about to set limits on his vexations of the good man, and so he rages extremely because his opportunity is short.

It is very remarkable that some of the greatest of the saints have died in the midst of the most fearful conflicts for the very same reason: the dog howled at them because he knew that they would soon be out of his reach.

You would not suppose that Martin Luther, a man so brave and strong that he could defy the Pope and the Devil, should on his deathbed be woefully unsure. Yet it was so: his worst struggle was the closing one. He was more than a conqueror (Romans 8:37), but the fight was severe, as if the Devil, that old coward, waited until he had his antagonist down, waited until he was weak and feeble, and then leaped upon him to vex him unmercifully, since he could not devour him.

Truly Luther had bothered the Devil, and we do not wonder at the malice of the Fiend. Satan knew that he would soon be out of the reach of his fiery arrows forever, and therefore he had to have a last shot at him.

It was precisely the same case with John Knox. Having been observed to sigh deeply and asked the cause of it, Knox replied thus:

> I have formerly, during my frail life, sustained many tests and many assaults of Satan, but at present he has

assailed me most fearfully, and put forth all his strength to devour, and make an end of me at once. Often before has he placed my sins before my eyes, often tempted me to despair, often endeavored to ensnare me by the allurements of the world; but these weapons were broken by the sword of the Spirit, the Word of God, and the Enemy failed. Now he has attacked me in another way: the cunning Serpent has labored to persuade me that I have merited heaven and eternal blessedness by the faithful discharge of my ministry. But, blessed be God, who has enabled me to beat down and quench this fiery dart by suggesting to me such passages of Scripture as these: *"What hast thou that thou didst not receive?"* (1 Corinthians 4:7) and *"By the grace of God I am what I am...not I, but the grace of God which was with me"* (1 Corinthians 15:10). Upon this, as one vanquished, he left me.

Wherefore I give thanks to my God through Jesus Christ, who has been pleased to give me the victory, and I am persuaded that the Tempter shall not again attack me, but, within a short time, I shall, without any great pain of body or anguish of mind, exchange this mortal and miserable life for a blessed immortality through Jesus Christ.

Do you wonder that the Devil was eager to have another knock at one who had given so many knocks to his dominion? Do not therefore be at all surprised if Satan rages against you, nor marvel if you yourself should seem to be given over to his power. Rather, rejoice in this, that his great wrath is the token of the shortness of his time. He wages war with us all the more cruelly because he knows that he will ultimately be defeated. His degraded mind delights in petty malice. If he cannot destroy, he will disturb. If he cannot kill, he will wound.

Subtle as he is, he acts foolishly in pursuing a hopeless object. In his war against any of the seed of the woman, he knows that he is doomed to defeat, yet he gnaws at the heel that breaks his head. It is the doom of evil to persevere in its spite after it knows that all is in vain—to be forever vanquished by the invincible Seed of the living God and yet forever to return to the fray. Sisyphus forever pushing upward a huge stone that rolls down on him is a true picture of the Devil vainly laboring to remove the truth from its place. Satan's efforts are indeed *"labour in vain"* (Galatians 4:11).

I want to call attention to one particular instance of this fact, which is seen in the soul who is coming to Christ, for whom Satan often has great wrath, knowing that his time is short. My object is to comfort those who are awakened and are seeking the Savior. If they are harassed, I desire that they may find peace, rest, and hope very quickly. When the poor man who was possessed with an evil spirit was being brought to Christ, we read that *"as he was yet a coming, the devil threw him down, and tare* [convulsed] *him"* (Luke 9:42). That is the way of the great Enemy: when he is about to be cast out, his energy is more displayed than ever, that if possible he may destroy the soul before it has obtained peace with God.

May the Comforter help me as I try to give encouragement on this subject.

Satan Knows His Time Is Short

Our first topic will be this: how does Satan know when his time is short with a person? He watches over all souls who are under his power with incessant maliciousness. He goes about the camp like a sentinel, spying out every man who is likely to be a deserter from his army.

In some men's hearts, the Deceiver dwells at ease, like a monarch in his palace.

Their minds are his favorite mansions. He goes in and out as he pleases and makes himself comfortably at home. He counts the man's nature as his own inheritance and works his own evil pleasure in him. Alas, the deceived man yields his members as instruments of unrighteousness and is willingly held enthralled. (See Romans 6:13.) All the man's faculties are the many chambers for Satan to dwell in, and his emotions are many fires and forges for Satan to work with.

Eventually, if divine grace intervenes, a change comes about. Satan, who has lived there twenty, thirty, forty, fifty, sixty years, begins to think that he will not be able to keep this residence of his much longer. He perceives that his time is short.

I suppose Satan perceives it first by discovering that he is not quite as welcome as he used to be. The man loved sin and found pleasure in it, but now sin is not as sweet as it was; its flavor is dull and insipid. The charms of vice are fading. Its pleasures are growing empty, vain, and void. This is an indication of a great change.

At one time, whenever a sin came near, the person kept an open house to entertain it with all hospitality, but now that soul is not as eager. Even the indwelling habitual lusts do not yield as much contentment as before, nor is as much provision made for them. The Black Prince and his court are out of favor, and this is a hint that they must soon be gone. When sin loses its sweetness, Satan is losing his power. The Adversary perceives that he must soon stretch his dragon wings when he sees that the indwelt heart is growing weary of him and is breaking away from his fascinations.

He grows more sure of his speedy ejection when he does not get the accommodation he used to have. The man was once eager for sin. He went in the pursuit of vice, hunted after it, and put himself in the way of temptation. Then Satan reigned securely. But now the man begins to forsake the haunts where sin walks openly. He abandons the cups of excitement that inflame the soul. You find him going to a place of worship and listening to a sermon, where before he frequented the taverns and enjoyed a sinful song at a music hall.

The Devil does not like this change and takes it as a warning that he will soon have to give up the key. The man does not drink or swear as he once did, nor does he readily yield himself up to every temptation. The fish is getting shy of the bait. The awakened man has not yet decided for Christ, but he is no longer at ease in bondage, no longer the glad slave of iniquity. He is on the wrong road, but he does not run on it. On the contrary, he pauses, heaves a sigh, and wishes he could leave the evil road, wishes he knew how to leap a hedge and get into the narrow way. Satan notices all of this, and he says to himself, "There is not the preparation made for me that there used to be. There is little readiness to run on my errands. Therefore, I perceive that my time is short."

Satan is still more convinced of the shortness of his possession of a man's heart when he hears knocking at that heart's door a hand whose power he has felt. He knows the kind of knock it is: a gentle but irresistible knocking upon the heart. Continual, perpetual, persevering is the knock of One who means to enter. The knock is by One who has a hole in His hand. He knocks not as one whose power lies in a blow, but as one whose tears and love are His battery of attack. His knock has an energy of compassion, an irresistibleness of gentle love. As Satan hears His knocking, when he perceives that the tenant of the house hears it, too, and is inclined to open the door, he is afraid. When the heart relents at the sound of the Gospel summons, he trembles more. If the knocking still continues, waking up the tenant in the dead of night, a sound heard amid the noise of traffic and above the laughter of fools, he says, "My time is short." He knows the hand that broke his head of old, and its knocking is ominous to him.

He knows that in the gentleness of Jesus there is an irresistible energy that must and will prevail. He therefore knows that his possession of the tenement is precarious when the Gospel is felt in the heart. Between the knocks he hears a voice that says, *"Open to me...for my head is filled with dew, and my locks with the drops of the night"* (Song 5:2), and he knows that this pleading voice bodes the downfall of his power.

Another indication to the Enemy that his time is short is when he knows that the tenant of the house steals away sometimes to court and asks for a warrant of eviction against him. You know what I mean—when the man feels that he cannot himself get rid of sin and cannot in his own strength conquer Satan, and therefore cries, "O God, help me. O God, for Christ's sake, drive out the old Dragon from my soul, I implore You." This is asking for a warrant of eviction. This is going to the court of heaven and pleading with the Great King to issue a summons and send His officer to eject the intruder, so that he may no longer pollute the spirit.

"Ah," says the Evil One, "this is not the place for me much longer, for, behold, he prays." More fierce than the flames of hell to Satan are the prayers of convicted sinners. When they pray, he must be gone. He must cry, "Retreat!" when men sound the trumpet of prayer. There is no staying in the camp any longer when the advance guard of prayer has come to take possession.

One more thing always makes Satan know that his time is short. That is when the Holy Spirit's power is evidently at work within the mind. Light has come in, and the sinner sees and knows what he was ignorant of before. Satan hates the light as much as he loves darkness. Like an owl in the daylight, he feels that he is out of place. Life comes in, too, by the Holy Spirit. The man feels, becomes sensitive, and becomes penitent. Satan, who loves death and always abides among the tombs, is bound to fly away from life. The Holy Spirit is beginning to work upon the man very graciously. Satan knows every throb of the Spirit's power, for it is the death of his power. So he says, "I will go to the place from where I came out, for this house trembles as if it were shaken with an earthquake and gives me no rest." Joyful tidings for a heart long tormented by this fierce Fiend! Away, Enemy; your destructions will soon come to a perpetual end!

Satan's Display of Rage

Inasmuch as the shortness of his tenure stirs up Satan's rage, we must next observe how he displays his great wrath. His fury rages differently in different people.

On some Satan displays his great wrath by stimulating outward persecution. The man is not a Christian yet, he is not actually converted yet, but Satan is so afraid that he will be saved that he sets all his dogs upon him. The poor soul goes into the workplace. Though he would give his eyes if he could say, "I am a Christian," he cannot quite say so. Nevertheless, his coworkers begin to pounce on him as much as if he were indeed one of the hated followers of Jesus. They scoff at him because he is serious and sober, because he is beginning to think and to be decent, because he is starting to listen to the Gospel and to care for the best things. Before the Christ child was born, the Dragon longed to devour Him. Before a man becomes a Christian, the Prince of the Power of the Air labors, if possible, to destroy him.

The Devil is determined not to lose anything by being behind. He begins as soon as grace begins. Now, if the grace of God is not in the awakened man, and his reformation is only a spasm of remorse, it is very likely that he will be driven back from all attention to the means of grace by the ribald remarks of the ungodly. However, if the Lord Jesus Christ has really been knocking at his door and the Spirit of God has begun to work, this opposition will not serve its purpose. The Lord will find wings for this poor soul so he may flee away from the trial that as yet he is not able to bear.

I have sometimes known such opposition even to tend to undo Satan's work and accomplish quite the opposite purpose. I know a man who was very troubled about the truth of Scriptures and about the doctrines of the Gospel, although he was a sincere searcher into the truth. He began to attend the church that I pastor and to listen to the Gospel, as an inquirer rather than as a believer. At that point, he could not state that he was a Christian, although he half wished he could. Now, it came to pass that the opposition he immediately received from the world strengthened his faith in the Bible and became a sort of missing link between him and the truth. The sneers of his comrades had this effect. He said to himself, "Why should they all attack me on the bare supposition of my being a Christian? If I had been a Muslim or a Jew, they would have regarded me with curiosity and let me alone. But inasmuch as they only suspect me of becoming a Christian, they are all down on me with contempt and anger. Now, why is this? Is not this a proof that I am right and that the Word of God is right, for did it not say that there should be enmity between the seed of the Serpent and the seed of the woman (Genesis 3:15)?"

The Devil did not know what he was doing when he opposed that young man and made a believer of him by that which was meant to drive him into unbelief. If the men of this world oppose the faith of our Lord Jesus Christ more fiercely than any other, surely it must be that there is something special in it, something opposed to their sinful ways or to their proud hopes, something that is of God. That was the inference that my young friend drew from the treatment he received, and that inference established him in the faith. Thus, you see,

Satan often hopes to save his dominion when his time is short through vehement persecution against the awakening sinner.

Much worse, however, is his other method of showing his wrath, namely, by vomiting floods out of his mouth to drown our newborn hope, if possible. When the hopeful hearer has not yet found peace and rest, Satan will sometimes try him with doubts, blasphemies, and temptations such as he never knew before. The tempted one has been amazed and has said to himself, "How is this? Can my desire for Christ be the work of God? I get worse and worse. I never felt as wicked as this until I began to seek a Savior." Yet this is no strange thing, fiery though the trial is.

Satan will suggest all the doubts he can about the inspiration of Scripture, the existence of God, the deity of Christ, and everything else that is revealed, until the poor heart that is earnestly longing for salvation will scarcely know whether there is anything true at all. The man will be so jumbled in his thoughts that he will hardly know whether he is on his head or his heels. *They reel to and fro, and stagger like a drunken man, and are at their wit's end"* (Psalm 107:27). The more they read the Bible and attend to the means of grace, the more they will be tempted to be skeptical and atheistic. Doubts they never knew before will torment them even while they strive to be devout.

The evil tenant has notice to leave, and he makes up his mind to do all the damage within his power while he is still within the doors. See how he breaks up precious truths and dashes down the richest hopes, and all with the detestable design of venting his spite upon the poor soul.

At such a time, Satan will also often arouse all the worst passions of our nature and drive them into unruly riot. The awakened sinner will be astonished as he finds himself harassed by temptations more base and foul than he has ever felt before. He will resist and strive against the assault, but it may be so violent that it staggers him. He can scarcely believe that the flesh is so utterly corrupt. The man who is anxiously seeking to go to heaven seems at such a time as if he were dragged down by seven strong demons to the eternal depths of perdition. He feels as if he had never known sin before or had been so completely beneath its power. The satanic troops sleep as if in a quiet garrison while the man is under the spell of sin, but once the heart is likely to be captured by Emmanuel's love, the infernal soldiers put on their worst manner and trample down all the thoughts and desires of the soul.

Satan may also attack the seeker in another form, with fierce accusations and judgments. He does not accuse some men, for he is quite sure that they are his very good friends. But when a man is likely to be lost to him, he alters his tone and threatens and condemns. He cries, "What, you be saved? It is impossible! You know what you used to be. Think of your past life." Then he rakes up a very hell before the man's eyes. "You!" he accuses. "Why, even since you have pretended to be a little better and have begun to attend to the means of grace, you know you have looked back with a longing eye and hungered for your old pleasures. It is quite out of the question that you should be a servant of Christ! He will not have such a ragamuffin as you in His house. The great Captain will never march at the head of a regiment that is disgraced by receiving such as you."

In *The Pilgrim's Progress*, Bunyan described Apollyon as standing across the road and swearing by his infernal den that the pilgrim should go no further. There would he spill his soul. Then he began to fling at him all types of fiery darts. Among them was this one: "Thou didst faint at first setting out, when thou wast almost choked in the gulf of Despond. Thou wast almost persuaded to go back at the sight of the Lions. Thou hast been false already to thy new Lord!"

Think for a moment of the Devil chiding us for sin! Oh, that the poor burdened soul could laugh at this hypocritical accuser, for he hates to be despised and yet he very well deserves it. Laugh at him, virgin daughter of Zion, for this great wrath of his is because his time is short. Who is he that he should bring an accusation against us? Let him mind himself. He has enough to answer for. When he turns to being an accuser, it is enough to make the child of God laugh him to scorn. Yet it is not easy to laugh when you are in this predicament, for the heart is ready to break with anguish.

Satan at such times has been known to pour into the poor troubled mind floods of blasphemy. I do not recollect as a child having heard blasphemy. Carefully brought up and kept out of harm's way, I think it could only have been once or twice that I ever heard profane language. Yet, when I was seeking the Lord, I distinctly remember the spot where the most hideous blasphemies that ever passed through the human mind rushed through my mind. I clapped my hands over my mouth for fear I would utter one of them. They were none of my inventing, nor had I revived them from my memory. They were the immediate suggestions of Satan himself, who was determined, if possible, to drive me to despair.

Read *Grace Abounding to the Chief of Sinners*, the story of John Bunyan's five years of torture under this particular misery, and you will see how Satan would say to him, "Sell Christ. Sell Christ. Give up Christ." As he went about his daily business, he would have it ringing in his ears, "Sell Christ. Sell Christ." When at last in a moment of torment, Bunyan thought he said, "Let Him go, if He will," then came the accusation, "Now it is all over with you. Jesus will have nothing to do with you, for you have given Him up. You are a Judas; you have sold your Lord." Then, when the poor man sought the Lord with tears and found peace again, some other dreadful insinuation would dog his heels. John Bunyan was at that time too precious a servant of the Devil for him to lose readily. The Enemy had perhaps some idea of what kind of servant of God the converted tinker would become and what sort of dreams Bunyan would have that would charm the hearts of many generations. Thus, Satan would not let him go without summoning all the tribes of hell to wreak their vengeance on him if they could not detain him in their service. Yet Bunyan escaped, and so will others in a similar case.

Oh, bond slave of the Devil, may you have grace to steal away to Jesus. Hasten away from Satan's power at once. Otherwise he will, as long as he has any opportunity, manifest his great wrath toward you.

How to Deal with Satan's Attacks

Our third consideration needs to be how we are to meet all of this. How must Satan be dealt with while he is showing his great wrath because his time is short?

First, if he is putting himself in this rage, let us get him out all the more quickly. If he remains quiet, even then we ought to be eager to be rid of his foul company. But if he shows this great rage, let us get him out right away. In God's name, let the Dragon be smitten if he is raving. If there is any opportunity of getting him out, back door or front door, do it right away; do not loiter or linger even for a single hour. A Devil raging, making us blaspheme and then accusing us, tempting us and betraying us, is such a dangerous occupant of a heart that he is not to be borne. Out he must go, and out at once. It is better to have a den of lions dwelling in our houses than the Devil within our hearts.

Lord, turn him out at once by Your own grace. We decide once and for all to wage war with him. We will linger no longer; we dare not. We will procrastinate no more; it is more than our lives are worth. Not tomorrow, but today, must the tyrant go. Not in a little while, but now, at this very moment, O Lord, drive the old Dragon from his throne with all his hellish crew!

That is the first advice I give you. Let the Enemy be cast out at once by divine grace.

The next thing is, inasmuch as we cannot get him out by our own unaided efforts, let us cry to the strong for strength, who can drive out this prince of the power of the air. There is life in a look at Jesus Christ. As soon as that life comes, away goes this Prince of Darkness as to his domination and reigning power. Oh, soul, there is nothing left for you but to look to Jesus Christ alone. Worried as you are and almost devoured, now is your time to put your trust in Jesus, who is mighty to save.

You know the text in Amos that speaks of the shepherd taking out of the lion's mouth two legs or a piece of an ear (Amos 3:12). The sheep was almost devoured, but still he pulled out from between the lion's jaws the last relics of his prey. If you seem to be reduced to two legs and a piece of an ear, still our glorious Shepherd can pull you out from between the lion's teeth and make you whole again, for He will not lose His sheep even at its last extremity.

What can you do against Satan? You would with pleasure be rid of him, but what can you do? Do nothing but this: cry to his Master against him. He may be mighty, but set the Almighty One upon him. He who accuses you, refer him to your Advocate. When he brings your sin before you, throw the blood of atonement in his face. Here is a text that will drive him down to his den: *"The blood of Jesus Christ his Son cleanseth us from all sin"* (1 John 1:7). Another is, *"This is a faithful saying, and worthy of all acceptation, that Christ Jesus came into the world to save sinners; of whom I am chief"* (1 Timothy 1:15). Quit battling with the wily Foe. Do not answer the old deceiver. If he tells you that you are a blasphemer, admit it. If he says you are utterly lost, acknowledge it. Then cast yourself at Jesus' feet, and He will overcome your Foe and set you free.

One more comfort for you is this: the more he rages, the more must your poor, troubled heart be encouraged to believe that he will soon be gone. I venture to say that nothing will make him go sooner than your full belief that he has to go. Courageous hope is a weapon that he dreads. Tell him he must be gone soon. He has been accusing you and pouring venom into your mind, making you believe that it is your blasphemy, when it is not yours but his. Say to him, "You will be gone soon. You may rage, but you will have to be gone."

"I have full possession of you," he says, "body and soul, and I triumph over you."

Respond to him, "And would you triumph over me as you do if you did not know that you will soon be driven out?"

"Ah," says he, "you will be lost, you will be lost." He howls at you as if ready to devour you.

Say to him, "If I was sure to be lost, you would not tell me so; you would sing sweet songs in my ears and lure me to destruction. You have to go; you know you do."

"Oh," says he, "it is impossible for you to be saved. You will be damned. You will have the hottest place in hell."

"But who sent you to tell me that?" you reply. "You have never spoken the truth yet. You are a liar from the beginning, and you are only saying this because you have to go. You know you have to go." Tell him so, and it is not long before he will depart. Say, *"Rejoice not against me, O mine enemy: when I fall, I shall arise"* (Micah 7:8).

Tell him you know his Master. Tell him he may nibble at your heel, but you recall the One who broke his head. Point to his broken head. He always tries to hide it if he can. Tell him his crown is battered to pieces, and tell him where that deed was done and by whose blessed hand.

As you tell him these things, he will shrink back. You will find yourself alone with Jesus only. Then will Jesus say to you, *"Where are those thine accusers?"* (John 8:10). You will look around and the Enemy will be gone. Then your blessed Master will say, *"Neither do I condemn thee: go, and sin no more"* (v. 11). May the Lord grant us such a riddance of our Archenemy this very moment for Christ's dear sake. Amen.

Three

Satanic Hindrances

Satan hindered us.
—1 Thessalonians 2:18

Paul, Silas, and Timothy were very desirous to visit the church at Thessalonica, but they were unable to do so for the singular reason announced in this text, namely, *"Satan hindered us."* It was not from lack of willingness, for they had a very great attachment to the Thessalonian believers, and they longed to look them in the face again. They said of the Thessalonians,

We give thanks to God always for you all,
making mention of you in our prayers;
Remembering without ceasing your work
of faith, and labour of love, and patience
of hope in our Lord Jesus Christ, in the
sight of God and our Father.
(1 Thessalonians 1:2–3)

Their desire to visit the church together was overruled, but being deeply concerned for its welfare, they sent Timothy alone to minister for a time in its midst. It was not lack of desire that hindered them, but lack of power.

They were not prevented by God's special providence. We find on certain occasions that Paul was not allowed to go precisely where his heart would have led him. *"They assayed to go into Bithynia: but the Spirit suffered them not"* (Acts 16:7). They *"were forbidden of the Holy Ghost to preach the word in Asia"* (v. 6); however, their course was directed toward Troas so that they might preach in Europe the unsearchable riches of Christ.

They could not, however, trace their absence from Thessalonica to any divine interdiction. It appeared to them to proceed from the great Adversary; *"Satan hindered them."* How Satan did so would be useless to state dogmatically, but we may form a reasonable conjecture. In the margin of my pulpit Bible is a note by one commentator that is probably correct: "Satan hindered Paul by raising such a storm of persecution against him at Berea and other places that it was deemed prudent to delay his visit until the storm was somewhat allayed."

However, I can hardly assume this to have been the only hindrance, for Paul was very courageous. Having a strong desire to visit Thessalonica, he would not have been kept away by fear of opposition. He did not shun the hottest part of the battle, but like a truly valiant champion, delighted most to be found in the thick of his foes. Possibly the antagonism of the various philosophers whom he met with at Athens and the evident heresies at Corinth, from which it seems that this epistle was written, may have called for his presence on the scene of action. He felt that he could not leave struggling churches to their enemies. He must contend with the grievous wolves and unmask the evil ones who wore the garb of angels of light.

Satan had moved the enemies of the truth to industrious opposition, and thus Paul and his companions were hindered from going to Thessalonica. It may have been that Satan had stirred up dissensions and discords in the churches that Paul was visiting, and therefore he was obliged to stop at one and then at another to settle their differences, to bring to bear the weight of his spiritual influence on the divided factions of the church to restore them to unity. Whether persecution, philosophic heresy, or division in the church was the outward instrument we cannot tell, but Satan was assuredly the prime mover.

You may wonder why the Devil cared so much about Paul and his whereabouts. Why did he take so much interest in keeping these three men from that particular church? This leads us to observe what wonderful importance is attached to the action of Christian ministers. Here was the Master of Evil, the Prince of the Power of the Air, intently watching the journeying of three humble men. And he was apparently far more concerned about their movements than about the actions of Nero or Tiberius. These despised heralds of mercy were his most dreaded foes. They preached the name that makes hell tremble. They declared that righteousness against which satanic hate always vents itself with its utmost power. With such malicious glances, the Archenemy watched their daily path. What cunning hands hindered them at all points!

It strikes me that Satan wanted to keep these apostolic men from the Thessalonican church because it was young and weak. Thus, he thought that if it was not fostered and helped by the preaching and presence of Paul, he might yet slay the young child. Moreover, for long ages he has had a fierce hatred of the preaching of the Gospel, and possibly there had been no public declaration of the truth throughout Thessalonica since Paul had gone. He was afraid lest the firebrands of the truth of the Gospel should again be flung in among the masses and a gracious conflagration should take place.

Besides, Satan always hates Christian fellowship. It is his policy to keep Christians apart. He delights in anything that can divide saints from one another. He attaches far more importance to godly relationships than we do. Since unity is strength, he does his best to promote separation. Thus, he kept Paul away from these believers, who might have gladdened his heart, and whose hearts he might have cheered. He would hinder their brotherly intimacy so that they might miss the strength that always flows from Christian communion and Christian sympathy.

This is not the only occasion in which Satan has hindered good men. Indeed, this has been his practice in all ages. We have selected this one particular incident so that some who are hindered by Satan may draw comfort from it, and so that we may have an opportunity (if the Spirit of God enables us) of saying a good and forceful word to any who think it is strange that this fiery trial has happened to them.

Satan's Habit of Hindrance

Let us observe that it has been Satan's practice from old to hinder, wherever he could, the work of God.

"Satan hindered us" is the testimony that all the saints in heaven will bear against the Archenemy. This is the witness of all who have written a holy line on the historic page or carved a consecrated name on the rock of immortality: *"Satan hindered us."*

In the sacred writings, we find Satan interfering in order to hinder the completion of the personal characters of individual saints. The man of Uz was blameless and upright before God and, to all appearances, would persevere in producing a finished picture of what the believer in God should be. Indeed, Job had so been enabled to live that the Archfiend could find no fault with his actions and only dared to impute wrong motives to him. Satan had considered Job, yet he could find no mischief in him.

But then the Fiend hinted, *"Hast not thou made an hedge about him, and about his house, and about all that he hath on every side?"* (Job 1:10). Satan sought to turn the blessing that Job was giving to God into a curse, and therefore he buffeted him severely. He stripped him of all his substance. The evil messengers followed on one another's heels, and their tidings of woe only ceased when his goods were all destroyed and his children had all perished. The poor afflicted parent was then struck in his bone and in his flesh until he was reduced to sitting on a dunghill and scraping himself with a piece of broken pottery. Even then the picture had no blot of sin upon it, and the ink pen was held with a steady hand by the patient saint.

Therefore Satan made another attempt to hinder Job's retaining his holy character. He stirred his wife to say, *"Dost thou still retain thine integrity? curse God, and die"* (Job 2:9). This was a great and grievous hindrance to the completion of Job's marvelous career, but glory be to God, the man of patience not only overcame Satan, but he also made him a stepping-stone to a yet greater height of illustrious virtue. You know about the patience of Job, which you would not have known if Satan had not illuminated it with the blaze of flaming afflictions. Had not the vessel been burnt in the furnace, the bright colors would not have been so fixed and abiding. The trial through which Job passed brought out the luster of his matchless endurance in submission and resignation to God.

Now, just as the Enemy waylaid and harassed the patriarch to hinder his perseverance in the path of excellence, so will he do with us. You may be congratulating yourself, saying, "I have walked consistently so far. No man can challenge my integrity." Beware of boasting, for your virtue will yet be tried. Satan will direct his forces against that very virtue for which you are the most famous. If you have been a firm believer up to this point, your faith will soon be attacked. If up until now you have been meek like Moses, expect to be tempted to speak unadvisedly with your lips. The birds will peck at your ripest fruit, and the wild boar will dash his tusks at your choicest vines.

Oh, if only we had among us more prominence of piety, more generosity of character, more faithfulness of behavior! In all these respects, I do not doubt, many of us have set out with the highest aims and intentions. Alas! How often have we had to cry, *"Satan hindered us!"*

This is not the Enemy's only business, for he is very earnest in endeavoring to hinder the emancipation of the Lord's redeemed ones. You know the memorable story of Moses. When the children of Israel were in captivity in Egypt, God's servant stood before their haughty oppressor with his rod in his hand. In Jehovah's name, he declared, *"Thus saith the LORD, Let my people go, that they may serve me"* (Exodus 8:1). A sign was required. The rod was cast upon the ground, and it became a serpent. At this point, Satan hindered. *"Jannes and Jambres withstood Moses"* (2 Timothy 3:8). We read that the magicians did the same thing with their enchantments. Whether it was by devilish arts or by sleight of hand, we need not fret over now. In either case, they did the Devil's dirty work, and they did it well, for Pharaoh's heart was hardened when he saw that the magicians apparently produced the same miracles as Moses had.

Beloved, take this as a type of Satan's hindrances to the Word of the Lord. Christ's servants came forth to preach the Gospel. Their ministry was accompanied by signs and wonders. "My kingdom is shaken," said the Prince of Evil; "I must get busy." Right away he sent magicians to work lying signs and wonders without number. Apocryphal wonders were and are as plentiful as the frogs of Egypt. Did the apostles preach the sacrifice of Christ? The Devil's apostles preached the sacrifice of the mass. Did the saints uplift the cross? The Devil's servants upheld the crucifix. Did God's ministers speak of Jesus as the one infallible Head of the church? The Devil's servants proclaimed the false priest of Rome as standing in that same place. Romanism is a most ingenious imitation of the Gospel. It is the *"magicians* [doing] *so with their enchantments"* (Exodus 8:7).

If you study well the genius spirit of the great Antichrist, you will see that its great power lies in its being an exceedingly clever counterfeit of the Gospel of the Lord Jesus Christ. To the extent that tinsel could counterfeit gold, candlelight could rival the sun in its glory, and a drop in a bucket could imitate the sea in its strength, the spirit of Antichrist has copied God's great masterpiece, the Gospel of our Lord Jesus Christ. To this day, as God's servants scatter the pure gold of truth, their worst enemies are those who issue worthless coins on which they have feloniously stamped the image and superscription of lying kings.

You have another case further on in history—all Old Testament history is typical of what is going on around us now. God was about to give a most wonderful system of instruction to Israel and to the human race, by way of type and ceremony, in the wilderness. Aaron and his sons were selected to represent the Great High Priest of our salvation, the Lord Jesus Christ. In every garment that they wore, there was a symbolic significance. Every vessel of that sanctuary in which they ministered taught a lesson. Every act of worship, whether it was the sprinkling of blood or the burning of incense, was made to teach precious and important truths to the sons of men. What a noble volume was unfolded in the wilderness at the foot of Sinai! How God declared Himself and the glory of the coming Messiah in the persons of Aaron and his sons!

What then? With this Satan interfered. Moses and Aaron could say, *"Satan hindered us."* Korah, Dathan, and Abiram arrogantly claimed a right to the priesthood. On a certain day, they stood with bronze censers in their hands, thrusting themselves impertinently into the office that the Lord had assigned to Aaron and to his sons. The earth opened and swallowed them up alive. (See Numbers 16:1–35.) This was a true prophecy of what will become of those who thrust themselves into the office of the priesthood where none but Jesus Christ can stand.

You may see the parallel today. Christ Jesus is the only priest who offered the sacrifice of blood, but no longer brings that sacrifice, for having once offered it, He has perfected forever those who are set apart (Hebrews 10:14). *"This man, after he had offered one sacrifice for sins for ever, sat down on the right hand of God"* (v. 12). Paul, with the strongest logic, proved that Christ does not offer a continual sacrifice, but that, having offered it once for all, His work was finished, and He now sits at the right hand of the Father.

This doctrine of a finished atonement and a completed sacrifice seemed likely to overrun the world. It was such a gracious unfolding of the divine mind that Satan could not look upon it without desiring to hinder it. Therefore, look on every hand, and you can see Korah, Dathan, and Abiram in those churches that are branches of the Anglican and the Roman. To this very day, men call themselves "priests" and read prayers from a book in which the catechism states, "Then shall the priest say...." These men falsely appropriate to themselves a priesthood other than that which is common to all the saints. Some of them even claim to offer a daily sacrifice, to celebrate an unbloody sacrifice at the place they call an altar. They claim to have power to forgive sin, saying to sick and dying persons, "By authority committed unto me, I absolve you from all your sins." This is the great hindrance to the propagation of the Gospel—the priestly pretensions of a set of men who are no priests of God, though they may be priests of Baal. Thus the ministers of Jesus are made to cry, *"Satan hinder[s] us."*

Take another instance of satanic hatred. When Joshua led the tribes across the Jordan, they were to attack the various cities that God had given them for a heritage. From Dan to Beersheba, the whole land was to be theirs. After the taking of Jericho, the first contact that they had with the heathen Canaanites ended in disastrous defeat to the servants of God; *"they fled before the men of Ai"* (Josh. 7:4). Here again you hear the cry, *"Satan hindered us."* Joshua might have gone from city to city exterminating the nations, as they justly deserved to be, but Achan had taken of the accursed thing and hidden it in his tent; therefore no victory could be won by Israel until his theft and sacrilege had been put away.

Beloved, this is symbolic of the Christian church. We might go from victory to victory, our home missions might be successful, and our foreign agencies might be crowned with triumph if we did not have an Achan in the home camp. When churches have no conversions, it is more than probable that hypocrites concealed among them have turned away the Lord's blessing. You who are inconsistent, who make the profession of religion the means of getting wealth, you who unite yourselves with God's people, but at the same time covet the costly Babylonian garment and the bar of gold, you are those who cut the muscles of Zion's strength. You prevent the Israel of God from going forth to victory. Little do we know how Satan has hindered us.

We, as the church, have had much reason to thank God. But how many more might have been added to the church if it had not been for the coldness of some, the indifference of others, the inconsistency of a few, and the worldliness of many more? Satan hinders us not merely by direct opposition, but by sending Achans into the midst of our camp.

I will give you one more picture. View the building of Jerusalem after it had been destroyed by the Babylonians. When Ezra and Nehemiah were found building, the Devil surely stirred up Sanballat and Tobiah to cast down. There was never a revival of religion without a revival of the old enmity. If ever the church of God is to be built, it will be in troubled times. When God's servants are active, Satan is not without vigilant followers who seek to counteract their efforts.

The history of the Old Testament church is a history of Satan endeavoring to hinder the work of the Lord. I am sure you will admit it has been the same since the days of the Lord Jesus Christ. When He was on earth, Satan hindered Him. Satan dared to attack Christ to His face personally. When that failed, Pharisees, Sadducees, Herodians, and men of all sorts hindered Him. When the apostles began their ministry, Herod and the Jews sought to hinder them. When persecution did not work, then all sorts of heresies and schisms broke out in the Christian church. Satan still hindered them. A very short time after the ascension of our Lord, the precious sons of Zion, comparable to fine gold, had become like earthen pitchers. The glory had departed and the luster of truth was gone because by false doctrine, lukewarmness, and worldliness, Satan hindered them.

When the Reformation dawned, God raised up a Luther, but the Devil brought out an Ignatius Loyola, founder of the Jesuits, to hinder him. If God had His reformers, His Latimers and His Wycliffes, the Devil had his opposers, his Gardiners and Bonners. When in the modern reformation Whitefield and Wesley thundered like the voice of God, there were ordained reprobates found to hinder them, to hold them up to reproach and shame.

Never, since the first hour struck in which goodness came into convict with evil, has it ceased to be true that Satan hindered us. From all points of the compass, all along the line of battle, in the vanguard and in the rear, at the dawn of day and at midnight, Satan hindered us. If we toil in the field, he seeks to break the plowshare. If we build the walls, he labors to cast down the stones. If we would serve God in suffering or in conflict, everywhere Satan hinders us.

Satan's Hindering Tactics

Next, we will examine the many ways in which Satan has hindered us.

The Prince of Evil is very busy in hindering those who are just coming to Jesus Christ. Here he spends the main portion of his skill. Some of us who know the Savior recollect the fierce conflicts that we had with Satan when we first looked to the Cross and lived.

Others of you are just passing through that trying season. I will address myself to you. Beloved friends, you long to be saved, but ever since you have given any attention to these eternal things, you have been the victim of deep distress of mind. Do not marvel at this. This is usual, so usual as to be almost universal.

I would wonder if you were not perplexed about the doctrine of election. The Enemy will suggest that you are not one of the chosen of God, although your common sense will teach you that it might just as well be suggested to you that you are, since you know neither the one nor the other, nor indeed can know until you have believed Jesus. Your present business is with the precept that is revealed, not with the election that is concealed. Your business is with the exhortation, *"Believe on the Lord Jesus Christ, and thou shalt be saved"* (Acts 16:31).

It is possible that the great fighting ground between predestination and free will may be the dry and desert place in which your soul is wandering. Now, you will never find any comfort there. The wisest of men have despaired of ever solving the mystery of those two matters, and it is not probable that you will find any peace in worrying yourself about it. Your business is not with metaphysical difficulty, but with faith in the atonement of the Lord Jesus Christ, which is simple and plain enough.

It is possible that your sins come to your remembrance, and though you once thought little enough of them, now it is hinted to you by satanic malice that they are too great to be pardoned. I urge you to reveal the lie of this by telling Satan this truth, that *"all manner of sin and blasphemy shall be forgiven unto men"* (Matthew 12:31).

However, the verse goes on to say that *"the blasphemy against the Holy Ghost shall not be forgiven unto men."* It is very likely that the sin against the Holy Spirit torments you a great deal. You read that *"unto him that blasphemeth against the Holy Ghost it shall not be forgiven"* (Luke 12:10). In this, too, you may be greatly tried. I wonder not that you are, for this is a most painfully difficult subject. One fact may cheer you: if you repent of your sins, you have not committed the unpardonable offense, since that sin necessitates hardness of heart forever. As long as a man has any tenderness of conscience and any softness of spirit, he has not so renounced the Holy Spirit as to have lost His presence.

It may be that you are the victim of blasphemous thoughts. Torrents of the filth of hell have been pouring through your soul. Do not be astonished at this, for there are some of us who delight in holiness and are pure in heart, who nevertheless have been sorely tried with thoughts that were never born in our hearts, but were injected into them. These suggestions are born in hell, not in our spirits. They are hated and loathed but are cast into our minds to hinder and trouble us.

Satan may hinder you as he did the child who was brought to Jesus. We read about him that as he *"was yet a coming, the devil threw him down, and tare him"* (Luke 9:42). Do come, nonetheless. Though seven demons were in him, Jesus would not cast the coming sinner out. Even if you feel a conviction that the unpardonable sin has fallen to your lot, yet dare to trust in Jesus. If you do that, I warrant you there will be a joy and a peace in believing that will overcome Satan, who has *"hindered us."*

But I must not stop long on any one point when there are so many. Satan is sure to hinder Christians when they are earnest in prayer. Have you not frequently found, dear friends, when you have been most earnest in supplication, that something or other will dart across your mind to make you cease from the exercise? It appears to me that we shake the tree and no fruit drops from it. Just when one more shake would bring down the luscious fruit, the Devil touches us on the shoulder and tells us it is time to be gone, and so we miss the blessing we might have attained. I mean that just when prayer would be the most successful, we are tempted to abstain from it. When my spirit has sometimes laid hold upon the angel, I have been painfully conscious of a counterinfluence urging me to cease from such petition and let the Lord alone, for His will would be done. If the temptation did not come in that shape, yet it came in another, to cease to pray because prayer after all could not avail. Oh, beloved, I know if you are much in prayer you can sing Cowper's hymn:

> That various hindrances we meet
> In coming to the mercy seat.

The same is true of Christians when under the prompting of the Spirit of God or when planning any good work. You were prompted to speak to someone. "Run, speak to that young man" was the message in your ear. You did not do it: Satan hindered you. You were told on a certain occasion—you do not know how, but believe me we ought to pay great respect to these inward whispers—to visit a certain person and help him. You did not do it: Satan hindered you. You were sitting down by the fire one evening reading a missionary report concerning Afghanistan or some area destitute of the truth. You thought, "Now I have a little money that I could give to this purpose." Then it came across your mind that there is another way of spending it more profitably for your family: so Satan hindered you. Or you yourself thought of doing a little in a certain district by way of preaching and teaching or some other form of Christian effort. As sure as you began to plan it, something or other arose, and Satan hindered you. If he possibly can, he will come upon God's people in those times when they are full of ardor and ready for Christian effort, in order to murder their infant plans and cast these suggestions of the Holy Spirit out of their minds.

How often, too, has Satan hindered us when we have entered into the work! In fact, beloved, we never ought to expect a success unless we hear the Devil making a noise. I have taken it as a certain sign that I am doing little good when the Devil is quiet. It is generally a sign that Christ's kingdom is coming when men begin to lie against you and slander you, casting about your name as evil.

Oh, those blessed storms! Do not give me calm weather when the air is still and heavy and when lethargy is creeping over one's spirit. Lord, send a hurricane. Give us a little stormy weather. When the lightning flashes and the thunder rolls, then God's servants know that the Lord is abroad, that His right hand is no longer kept inactive, that the moral atmosphere will get clear, that God's kingdom will come and His will be done on earth, even as it is in heaven.

"Peace, peace, peace," the Dragon's wings flap. The stern voice that proclaims perpetual war is the voice of the Captain of our salvation. You ask, "How is this?"

> *Think not that I am come to send peace on earth: I came not to send peace, but a sword.*
> *For I am come to set a man at variance against his father, and the daughter against her mother, and the daughter in law against her mother in law.*
> *And a man's foes shall be they of his own household.* (Matthew 10:34–36)

Christ does make physical peace. There is to be no strife with the fist, no blow with the sword. But moral and spiritual peace can never exist in this world where Jesus Christ is, as long as error is there.

You know, beloved, that you cannot do any good thing without the Devil being sure to hinder you. What then? Up and at him! Cowardly looks and faint counsels are not for warriors of the Cross. Expect fighting and you will not be disappointed. Whitefield used to say that some ministers would go from the first of January to the end of December with a perfectly whole skin. The Devil never thought them worth attacking. But let us begin to preach the Gospel of Jesus Christ with all our might and soul and strength, and men will soon begin laughing at us and ridiculing us. If they do, so much the better. We are not alarmed because Satan hinders us.

Nor will he only hinder us in working. He will hinder us in seeking to unite with one another. We are about to make an effort, as Christian churches in London, to come closer together, and I am happy to find indications of success. But I should not be amazed if Satan hinders us, and I ask your prayers that Satan may be routed in this matter and that the union of our churches may be accomplished. In my church, we have walked together in peace for a long time, but I should not marvel if Satan tries to hinder our walking in love, peace, and unity.

Satan will hinder us in our communion with Jesus Christ. When at His table, we think to ourselves, "I will have a sweet moment now," just then vanity intrudes. Like Abraham, you offer the sacrifice, but the unclean birds come down upon it, and you need to drive them away. *"Satan hindered us."* He is not omnipresent, but by his numerous servants, he works in all kinds of places and manages to distract the saints when they would serve the Lord.

Rules for Discernment

In the third place, there are two or three rules by which these hindrances may be detected as satanic.

I think I hear somebody saying to himself, "I would have risen in the world and would be a wealthy man now if Satan had not hindered me." Do not believe it, dear friend. I do not believe that Satan generally hinders people from getting rich. He would just as soon have them be rich as poor. He delights to see God's servants set upon the pinnacle of the temple, for he knows the position to be dangerous. High places and God's praise seldom well agree. If you have been hindered in growing rich, I should rather set that down to the good providence of God that would not place you where you could not have borne the temptation.

"Yes," said another, "I intended to live in a certain neighborhood and do well but have not been able to go. Perhaps that is the Devil." Perhaps it is. Perhaps it is not. God's providence knows best where to place us. We are not always able to choose our own locality. We are not always to conclude when we are hindered and disappointed in our own intentions that Satan has done it, for it may very often be the good providence of God.

But how may I tell when Satan hinders me? I think you may tell, first, by the purpose. Satan's object in hindering us is to prevent our glorifying God. If anything has happened to you that has prevented your growing holy, useful, humble, and sanctified, then you may trace that to Satan. If the distinct object of the interference to the general current of your life has been that you may be turned from righteousness to sin, then from the objective you may guess the author. It is not God who does this;

rather Satan does. Yet, know that God does sometimes put apparent hindrances in the way of His own people, even in regard to their usefulness and growth in grace. But His objective is still to be considered: it is to try His saints and so to strengthen them. The purpose of Satan is to turn them from the right road and make them take the crooked way.

You may tell the suggestions of Satan, again, by the method in which they come: God employs good motives, Satan bad ones. If what has turned your attention away from your the Lord has been a bad thought, a bad doctrine, a bad teaching, a bad motive—that never came from God; that must be from Satan.

Again, you may tell the suggestions from their nature. Whenever an impediment to usefulness is pleasing or gratifying to you, consider that it came from Satan. Satan never brushes the feathers of his birds the wrong way. He generally deals with us according to our tastes and likes. He flavors his bait to his fish. He knows exactly how to deal with each man and how to use the motive that will fall in line with the suggestions of the carnal nature. If the difficulty in your way is rather contrary to yourself than for yourself, then it comes from God. If what now is a hindrance brings you gain, pleasure, or advantage in any way, rest assured it came from Satan.

We can tell the suggestions of Satan, once more, by their season. Hindrances to prayer, for instance, if they are satanic, come out of the natural course and relation of human thoughts. It is a law of the mind that one thought suggests another, which suggests the next, and so on, as the links of a chain are one after the other. But satanic temptations do not come in the regular order of thinking: they dash upon the mind unexpectedly. My soul is in prayer, so it would be unnatural that I should then blaspheme, yet then the blasphemy comes. Therefore it is clearly satanic and not from my own mind. If I am set upon doing my Master's will but a cowardly thought assails me, that idea, which differs from the natural bent of my mind and thoughts, may be at once ejected as not being mine and may be set down to the account of the Devil, who is the true father of it.

By these means I think we may tell when Satan hinders, when the hindrance is our own heart, or when it is of God. We ought to carefully watch that we do not put the saddle on the wrong horse. Do not blame the Devil when it is yourself. On the other hand, when the Lord puts a bar in your way, do not attribute this to Satan and so go against God's providence. It may be difficult at times to see the way, but if you go to the throne of God in prayer, you will soon discover it. *"Bring hither the ephod"* (1 Samuel 23:9), said David when he was in difficulty. Do you say the same? Go to the Great High Priest, whose business it is to give forth the oracle! Upon His chest hangs the Urim and Thummim, and you will find direction from Him in every time of difficulty and dilemma.

Acting against Hindrances

Supposing that we have ascertained that hindrances in our way really have come from Satan, what do we do then? I have but one piece of advice, and that is to go on, hindrance or no hindrance, in the path of duty as God the Holy Spirit enables you.

If Satan hinders you, I have already hinted that this opposition should cheer you. "I did not expect," said a Christian minister, "the work to be easy in this particular pastorate, or else I would not have come here. I always count it my duty to show the Devil that I am his enemy, and if I do that, I expect that he will show me that he is mine." If you are now opposed and you can trace that opposition distinctly to Satan, congratulate yourself upon it. Do not sit down and fret. Why, it is a great thing that a poor creature like you can actually vex the great Prince of Darkness and win his hate. It makes the race of man the more noble when it comes in conflict with a race of spirits and stands toe to toe even with the Prince of Darkness himself.

It is a dreadful thing, undoubtedly, that you should be hindered by such an adversary, but it is most hopeful, for if he were your friend, you might have cause to fear indeed. Stand up against him, because you now have an opportunity of making a greater gain than you could have had if he had been quiet. You could never have had a victory over him if you had not engaged in conflict with him. The poor saint would go on his inglorious way to heaven if he were untempted, but being tormented, every step of his pathway becomes glorious. Our position today is like that described by Bunyan in *The Pilgrim's Progress,* when from the top of the palace the song was heard:

Come in, come in,
Eternal glory thou shalt win.

Now merely to ascend the stairs of the palace, though safe work, would not have been very ennobling. However, when the foes crowded around the door and blocked every stair, the hero came to the man with the inkstand, who sat in front of the door, and said, "Write my name down, sir." Then to get from the lowest step to the top where the bright ones were singing made every inch glorious. If devils did not oppose my path from earth to heaven, I might travel joyously, peacefully, safely, but certainly without renown. But now, when every step is contested in winning our pathway to glory, every single step is covered with immortal fame. Press on then, Christian. The more opposition, the more honor.

Be in earnest against these hindrances when you consider what you lose if you do not resist and overcome him. To allow Satan to overcome me would be eternal ruin to my soul. Certainly it would forever blast all hopes of my usefulness. If I retreat and turn my back in the day of battle, what will the rest of God's servants say? What shouts of derision would ring over the battlefield! How the banner of the covenant would be trailed in the mire! Why, we must not, we dare not, play the coward. We dare not give way to the insinuation of Satan and turn from the Master, for the defeat would then be too dreadful to be endured.

Beloved, let me feed your courage with the recollection that your Lord and Master has overcome. See Him there before you. He of the crown of thorns has fought the Enemy and broken his head. Satan has been completely vanquished by the Captain of your salvation. That victory was representative—He fought and won it for you.

You have to contend with a defeated Foe, one who knows and feels his disgrace. Though he may fight with desperation, yet he does not fight with true courage, for he is hopeless of ultimate victory. Strike, then, for Christ has smitten him. Down with him, for Jesus has had him under His foot. You, weakest of all the host, triumph, for the Captain has triumphed before you.

Lastly, remember that you have a promise to help you prepare for battle and be courageous this day. *"Resist the devil, and he will flee from you"* (James 4:7). Christian minister, do not resign. Do not think of sending in your resignation because the church is divided and the Enemy is making headway. Resist the Devil. Flee not, but make him flee. Christian young men, you who have begun to preach in the street, distribute tracts, or visit from house to house, though Satan hinders you very much, I urge you to redouble your efforts. It is because Satan is afraid of you that he resists you, because he would rob you of the great blessing that is now descending on your head. Resist him, and stand fast. You who are pleading in prayer, do not let go of your hold upon the covenant angel now. Satan is hindering you now because the blessing is descending. You are seeking Christ, so do not close those eyes or turn away your face from Calvary's streaming tree. Now that Satan hinders you, it is because the night is almost over and the day star begins to shine. Beloved, you who are most tormented, most sorrowfully tried, most weighed down, yours is the brighter hope. Be courageous. Play the warrior for God, for Christ, for your own soul. The day will come when you will ride triumphant through the streets of the New Jerusalem with your Master—with sin, death, and hell captive at your chariot wheels. and you with your Lord crowned as victor, having overcome through the blood of the Lamb.

May God bless you, dear friends. I do not know to whom this chapter may be most suitable, but I believe it is sent especially to certain tried saints. May the Lord enable them to find comfort in it. Amen.

Four

Christ, the Conqueror
of Satan

And I will put enmity between thee and the woman,
and between thy seed and her seed;
it shall bruise thy head,
and thou shalt bruise his heel.
—*Genesis 3:15*

This is the first gospel sermon that
was ever delivered on this earth. It
was a memorable discourse indeed,
with Jehovah Himself for the preacher, and
the whole human race and the Prince of

Darkness for the audience. It must be worthy of our heartiest attention.

Is it not remarkable that this great gospel promise should have been delivered so soon after the transgression? As yet no sentence had been pronounced upon either of the two human offenders, but the promise was given under the form of a sentence pronounced upon the Serpent. Not yet had the woman been condemned to painful travail, or the man to exhausting labor, or even the soil to the curse of thorn and thistle. Truly *"mercy rejoiceth against judgment"* (James 2:13). Before the Lord had said, *"Dust thou art, and unto dust shalt thou return"* (Genesis 3:19), He was pleased to say that the Seed of the woman would bruise the Serpent's head. Let us rejoice, then, in the swift mercy of God, which in the early watches of the night of sin, came with comforting words to us.

These words were not directly spoken to Adam and Eve, but they were directed distinctly to the Serpent himself, and that by way of punishment to him for what he had done. It was a day of cruel triumph to him. Such joy as his dark mind is capable of had filled him, for he had indulged his malice and gratified his spite. He had in the worst sense destroyed a part of God's works. He had introduced sin into the new world, had stamped the human race with his own image, and had gained new forces to promote rebellion and to multiply transgression. Thus he felt the sort of gladness that a fiend can know who bears a hell within him.

But now God comes in, takes up the quarrel personally, and causes him to be disgraced on the very battlefield upon which he had gained a temporary success. He tells the Dragon that He will undertake to deal with him; this quarrel would not be between the Serpent and man, but between God and the Serpent. God says, in solemn words, *"I will put enmity between thee and the woman, and between thy seed and her seed."* He promises that there will rise in fullness of time a champion who, though He may suffer, will smite the power of evil in a vital part by bruising the Serpent's head. It seems to me that this was the more comforting message of mercy to Adam and Eve, because they could feel sure that the Tempter would be punished, and since that punishment would involve blessing for them, the vengeance due to the Serpent would be the guarantee of mercy to themselves.

Perhaps, however, by thus indirectly giving the promise, the Lord meant to say,

"Not for your sakes do I this, fallen man and woman, nor for the sake of your descendants. Rather, for My own name and honor's sake, that it be not profaned and blasphemed among the fallen spirits. I undertake to repair the mischief that has been caused by the Tempter, that My name and My glory may not be diminished among the immortal spirits who look down upon the scene." All this was very humbling but yet consolatory to our parents if they thought of it, seeing that mercy given for God's sake is always to our troubled apprehension more sure than any favor that could be promised to us for our own sakes. The divine sovereignty and glory afford us a stronger foundation of hope than merit, even if merit could be supposed to exist.

Now we must note concerning this first gospel sermon that on it the earliest believers steadied themselves. This was all that Adam had by way of revelation, and all that Abel had received. This one lone star shone in Abel's sky; he looked up to it and believed. By its light he spelled out "sacrifice," and thus he brought of the firstlings of his flock and laid them upon the altar. He proved in his own person how the seed of the Serpent hated the seed of the woman, for his brother killed him for his testimony.

Although Enoch, the seventh generation from Adam, prophesied concerning the Second Advent (see Jude 1:14–15), yet he does not appear to have uttered anything new concerning the first coming, so that still this one promise remained as man's sole word of hope. The torch that flamed within the gates of Eden just before man was driven forth lit up the world to all believers until the Lord was pleased to give more light, and to renew and enlarge the revelation of His covenant, when He spoke to His servant Noah.

Those silvery-haired fathers who lived before the Flood rejoiced in the mysterious language of our text. Resting on it, they died in faith. Nor, beloved, must you think it a slender revelation, for it is wonderfully full of meaning if you attentively consider it. If it had been on my heart to handle it doctrinally this morning, I think I could have shown you that it contains the whole Gospel. There lie within it, as an oak lies within an acorn, all the great truths that make up the Gospel of Christ.

Observe that here is the grand mystery of the incarnation. Christ is that Seed of the woman who is spoken of here. There is a broad hint as to how that incarnation would be brought about. Jesus was not born after the ordinary manner of the sons of men. Mary was overshadowed by the Holy Spirit, and the Holy One that was born of her was, concerning His humanity, the seed of the woman only. As it is written, *"Behold, a virgin shall conceive, and bear a son, and shall call his name Immanuel"* (Isaiah 7:14). The promise plainly teaches that the Deliverer would be born of a woman. Viewed carefully, it also foreshadows the divine method of the Redeemer's conception and birth.

The doctrine of the two seeds is also plainly taught here: *"I will put enmity between thee and the woman, and between thy seed and her seed."* There was evidently to be in the world a seed of the woman on God's side against the Serpent, and a seed of the Serpent that would always be on the evil side, even as it is to this day. The church of God and the temple of Satan both exist. We see an Abel and a Cain, an Isaac and an Ishmael, a Jacob and an Esau. Those who are born after the flesh are the children of their father the Devil, for they do his works. But those who are born again, being born of the Spirit after the power of the life of Christ, are thus in Christ Jesus the seed of the woman, and contend earnestly against the Dragon and his seed.

Here, too, the great fact of the sufferings of Christ is foretold clearly: *"Thou shalt bruise his heel."* Within those words, we find the whole story of our Lord's sorrows from Bethlehem to Calvary.

"It shall bruise thy head." Here is the breaking of Satan's regal power; here is the clearing away of sin; here is the destruction of death by resurrection; here is the leading of captivity captive in the Ascension; here is the victory of truth in the world through the descent of the Spirit; here is the latter-day glory in which Satan will be bound; and lastly, here is the casting of the Evil One and all his followers into the lake of fire. The conflict and the conquest are both encompassed by these few fruitful words.

The words may not have been fully understood by those who first heard them, but to us they are now full of light. The text at first looks like a flint, hard and cold; but sparks fly from it plentifully, because hidden fires of infinite love and grace lie concealed within. Over this promise of a gracious God, we ought to rejoice greatly.

We do not know what our first parents understood by these words, but we may be certain that they gathered a great amount of comfort from them. They must have understood that they were not then and there to be destroyed, because the Lord had spoken of a *"seed."* They could reason that it must be that Eve would live if there would be a seed from her. They understood, too, that if that Seed was to overcome the Serpent and bruise his head, it must herald good to themselves: they could not fail to see that there was some great, mysterious benefit to be conferred upon them by the victory that their Seed would achieve over the instigator of their ruin. They continued on in faith upon this, and were comforted in travail and in toil. I do not doubt that both Adam and his wife, in this faith, entered into everlasting rest.

I intend to handle this text in three ways. First, we will notice its facts. Then, we will consider the experience within the heart of each believer that attests to those facts. Finally, we will find the encouragement that the text and its connection as a whole afford to us.

The Facts

The facts are four, and I call your earnest attention to them. The first is that enmity was stirred up. The text begins, *"I will put enmity between thee and the woman."* The woman and the Serpent had been very friendly. They had conversed together. She thought at the time that the Serpent was her friend. She was so much his friend that she took his advice in the face of God's precept and was willing to believe bad things of the great Creator because this wicked, crafty Serpent insinuated the same. Now, at the moment that God spoke, that friendship between the woman and the Serpent had already in a measure come to an end, for she had accused the Serpent to God by saying, *"The serpent beguiled me, and I did eat"* (Genesis 3:13). So far, so good. The friendship of sinners does not last long. Eve and the Serpent had already begun to quarrel. Then the Lord came in and graciously took advantage of the quarrel and said, "I will carry this disagreement a great deal further. I will put enmity between the Serpent and the woman."

Satan counted on man's descendants being his allies, but God would break up this covenant with hell and raise up a Seed that would war against the satanic power. Thus we have here God's first declaration that He would set up a rival kingdom to oppose the tyranny of sin and Satan, that He would create in the hearts of a chosen seed an enmity against evil so that they would fight against it, and with many a struggle and pain would overcome the Prince of Darkness. The divine Spirit has abundantly achieved this plan and purpose of the Lord, combating the Fallen Angel by a glorious man, making man to be Satan's foe and conqueror.

From this point onward, the woman was to hate the Evil One, and I do not doubt that she did so. She had abundant cause for doing so. As often as she thought of him, it would be with infinite regret that she could have listened to his malicious and deceitful talk. The woman's seed has also evermore had enmity against the Evil One. I do not mean the carnal seed, for Paul tells us, *They which are the children of the flesh, these are not the children of God: but the children of the promise are counted for the seed*" (Romans 9:8). I do not mean the carnal seed of the man and the woman, but rather the spiritual seed, even Christ Jesus and those who are in Him. Wherever you meet these, they hate the Serpent with a perfect hatred. We would if we could destroy from our souls every work of Satan, and out of this poor afflicted world of ours we would root up every evil that he has planted.

That glorious Seed of the woman—for God did not speak of many seeds, but of one Seed—you know how He abhorred the Devil and all his devices. There was enmity between Christ and Satan, for He came to destroy the works of the Devil and to deliver those who are under bondage to him. For that purpose was He born in the flesh; for that purpose did He live; for that purpose did He die; for that purpose He has gone into glory; and for that purpose He will come again, that everywhere He may root out His Adversary and utterly destroy him and his works from among the sons of men.

Putting enmity between the two seeds was the commencement of the plan of mercy, the first act in the program of grace. Of the woman's seed it was henceforth said, *"Thou lovest righteousness, and hatest wickedness: therefore God, thy God, hath anointed thee with the oil of gladness above thy fellows"* (Psalm 45:7).

The second prophecy, which has also turned into a fact, concerns the coming of the Champion. The Seed of the woman by promise is to champion the cause and oppose the Dragon. That Seed is the Lord Jesus Christ. The prophet Micah said,

> *But thou, Bethlehem Ephratah, though thou be little among the thousands of Judah, yet out of thee shall he come*

> *forth unto me that is to be ruler in Israel;*
> *whose goings forth have been from of*
> *old, from everlasting.*
> *Therefore will he give them up, until the*
> *time that she which travaileth hath*
> *brought forth.* (Micah 5:2–3)

To none other than the Babe who was born in Bethlehem of the blessed virgin can these words of prophecy refer. She it was who conceived and bore a Son. Concerning her Son we sing, *"For unto us a child is born, unto us a son is given: and the government shall be upon his shoulder: and his name shall be called Wonderful, Counsellor, The mighty God, The everlasting Father, The Prince of Peace"* (Isaiah 9:6). One memorable night at Bethlehem, when angels sang in heaven, the Seed of the woman appeared. As soon as he saw the light, the old Serpent, the Devil, planted into the heart of Herod the desire to slay Jesus, but the Father preserved Him and allowed none to lay hands on Him.

As soon as Jesus publicly came forward upon the stage of action, thirty years later, Satan met Him toe to toe. You know the story of the temptation in the wilderness, and how there the woman's Seed fought with him who had been a liar from the beginning. The Devil assailed Him three times with all the artillery of flattery, malice, craft, and falsehood, but the peerless Champion stood unwounded and chased His foe from the field. Then our Lord set up His kingdom, called one and another unto Himself, and carried the war into the Enemy's country. In many places He cast out devils. He spoke to the wicked, unclean spirit, *"Thou dumb and deaf spirit, I charge thee, come out of him"* (Mark 9:25), and the demon was expelled. Legions of devils flew before Him; they sought to hide themselves in swine to escape from the terror of His presence. *"Art thou come hither to torment us before the time?"* (Matthew 8:29) was their cry when the wonder-working Christ dislodged them from the bodies that they tormented. He made His own disciples mighty against the Evil One, for in His name they cast out devils, until Jesus said, *"I beheld Satan as lightning fall from heaven"* (Luke 10:18).

Then there came a second personal conflict, for I take it that Gethsemane's sorrows were to a great degree caused by a personal assault of Satan, for our Master said, *"This is your hour, and the power of darkness"* (Luke 22:53). He said also, *"The prince of this world cometh, and hath nothing in me"* (John 14:30). What a struggle it was!

Though Satan had nothing in Christ, yet he sought if possible to lead Him away from completing His great sacrifice. There our Master's *sweat was as it were great drops of blood falling down to the ground* (Luke 22:44) in the agony that it cost Him to contend with the Fiend. Then it was that our Champion began the last fight of all and won it to the bruising of the Serpent's head. Nor did He end until He had spoiled principalities and powers and made a show of them openly.

> Now is the hour of darkness past,
> Christ has assumed His reigning power;
> Behold the great accuser cast
> Down from his seat to reign no more.

The conflict of our glorious Lord continues in His seed. We preach Christ crucified, and every sermon shakes the gates of hell. We bring sinners to Jesus by the Spirit's power, and every convert is a stone torn down from the wall of Satan's mighty castle. Yes, the day will come when everywhere the Evil One will be overcome, and the words of John in Revelation will be fulfilled:

> *The great dragon was cast out, that old serpent, called the Devil, and Satan, which deceiveth the whole world....*

And I heard a loud voice saying in heaven, Now is come salvation, and strength, and the kingdom of our God, and the power of his Christ: for the accuser of our brethren is cast down, which accused them before our God day and night. (Revelation 12:9–10)

Thus did the Lord God in the words of our text promise a Champion who would be the Seed of the woman, between whom and Satan there would be war forever and ever. That Champion has come; the Man-child has been born. Though the Dragon is raging with the woman and makes war with the remnant of her seed that keep the testimony of Jesus Christ, yet the battle is the Lord's, and the victory falls to Him whose name is *"Faithful and True, and in righteousness he doth judge and make war"* (Revelation 19:11).

The third fact that comes out in the text, though not quite in that order, is that our Champion's heel would be bruised. Do you need me to explain this? You know how all through Christ's life His heel—that is, His lower part, His human nature—was perpetually being made to suffer. He carried our sicknesses and sorrows. But the bruising came mainly when, both in body and in mind, His whole human nature was made to agonize, when His soul was exceedingly sorrowful even unto death, when His enemies pierced His hands and His feet, and when He endured the shame and pain of death by crucifixion.

Look at your Master and your King on the cross, all stained with blood and dust! There was His heel most cruelly bruised. When they took down that precious body, wrapped it in fair white linen and in spices, and laid it in Joseph's tomb, they wept as they handled that casket in which the Deity had dwelt, for there again Satan had bruised His heel. It was not merely that God had bruised Him, *"yet it pleased the LORD to bruise him"* (Isaiah 53:10). But the Devil had let loose Herod, Pilate, Caiaphas, the Jews, and the Romans—all of them his tools—upon Him whom he knew to be the Christ, so that He was bruised by the old Serpent.

That is all, however! It was only His heel, not His head, that was bruised! The Champion rose again. The bruise was not mortal or continual. Though He died, still so brief was the interval in which He slumbered in the tomb that His holy body did not see corruption, and He came forth perfect and lovely in His manhood, rising from His grave as from a refreshing sleep after a long day of unresting toil! Oh, the triumph of that hour! As Jacob only limped with his injured hip when he overcame the angel, so Jesus was only scarred in His heel, and that He bears in the skies as His glory and beauty. Before the throne He looks like a lamb that has been slain, but in the power of an endless life He lives unto God.

Then comes the fourth fact, namely, that while His heel was being bruised, He was to bruise the Serpent's head. The figure represents the Dragon as inflicting an injury upon the Champion's heel, but at the same moment the Champion Himself with that heel crushes the head of the Serpent with fatal effect. By His sufferings Christ has overthrown Satan; by the heel that was bruised He has trodden upon the head that devised the bruising.

> Lo, by the sons of hell He dies;
> But as He hangs 'twixt earth and skies,
> He gives their prince a fatal blow,
> And triumphs o'er the powers below.

Although Satan is not dead, my beloved—I was about to say, I would to God that he were—although he is not converted and never will be, nor will the malice of his heart ever be driven from him, yet Christ has so far broken his head that he has missed his mark altogether. He intended to make the human race the captives of his power, but they are redeemed from his iron yoke. God has delivered many of them, and the day will come when He will cleanse the whole earth from the Serpent's slimy trail, so that the entire world will be full of the praises of God.

Satan thought that this world would be the arena of his victory over God and good. Instead, it is already the grandest theater of divine wisdom, love, grace, and power. Heaven itself is not so resplendent with mercy as the earth is, for it is here that the Savior poured out His blood.

No doubt, he thought that when he had led our race astray and brought death upon us, he had effectually marred the Lord's work. He rejoiced that we would all pass under the cold seal of death, and that our bodies would rot in the sepulcher. Had he not spoiled the handiwork of his great Lord? God may make man as a curious creature with intertwined veins and nerves, tendons and muscles, and He may put into his nostrils the breath of life. Yet, Satan says, "I have infused a poison into him that will make him return to the dust from which he was taken."

But now, behold, our Champion whose heel was bruised has risen from the dead and given us a solemn pledge that all of His followers will rise from the dead also. Thus Satan was foiled, because death will not retain a bone, nor a piece of a bone, of one of those who belonged to the woman's seed. At the trump of the archangel, from the earth and from the sea, we will arise, and this will be our shout: *"O death, where is thy sting? O grave, where is thy victory?"* (1 Corinthians 15:55). Satan, knowing this, feels already that his head is broken by the resurrection. Glory be to the Christ of God for this!

In multitudes of other ways, the Devil has been vanquished by our Lord Jesus, and so will he ever be until he is cast into the lake of fire.

Comparing Our Experiences

Let us now view our experiences as they correspond to these facts. Now, brothers and sisters, we were by nature, those of us who have been saved, the heirs of wrath even as others. Regardless of how godly our parents were, the first birth brought us no spiritual life, for the promise is to them *"which were born, not of blood, nor of the will of the flesh, nor of the will of man, but* [only to those who are born] *of God"* (John 1:13). *"That which is born of the flesh is flesh"* (John 3:6); you cannot make it anything else. The flesh, or carnal mind, abides in death; it is not reconciled to God, nor indeed can it be. He who is born into this world but once, and knows nothing of the new birth, must place himself among the seed of the Serpent, for only by regeneration can we know ourselves to be the true seed.

How does God deal with us who are His called and chosen ones? He means to save us, and how does He work to that end? The first thing He does is that He comes to us in mercy and puts enmity between us and the Serpent. That is the very first work of grace. There was peace between us and Satan once. When he tempted, we yielded. Whatever he taught us, we believed. We were his willing slaves.

But perhaps you can recall when you first began to feel uneasy and dissatisfied. The world's pleasures no longer pleased you. All the juice seemed to have been taken out of the apple, and you had nothing left but the hard core, which you could not eat at all. Then you suddenly perceived that you were living in sin, and you were miserable about it. Though you could not get rid of sin, you hated it, sighed over it, and cried and groaned. In your heart of hearts, you remained no longer on the side of evil, for you began to cry, *"O wretched man that I am! who shall deliver me from the body of this death?"* (Romans 7:24).

In the covenant of grace of old, you were already ordained to be the woman's seed, and now the decree began to discover itself in life bestowed upon you and working in you. The Lord in infinite mercy dropped the divine life into your soul. You did not know it, but there it was, a spark of the celestial fire, the living and incorruptible seed that abides forever. You began to hate sin, and you groaned under it as under an irritating yoke. More and more it burdened you; you could not bear it, and you hated the very thought of it.

So it was with you. Is it so now? Is there still enmity between you and the Serpent? Indeed, you are more and more the sworn enemies of evil, and you willingly acknowledge it.

Then came the Champion; that is to say, *"Christ in you, the hope of glory"* (Colossians 1:27) was formed. You heard of Him and understood the truth about Him. It seemed a wonderful thing that He would be your substitute and stand in your place, that He would bear your sin and all its curse and punishment, and that He should give His righteousness and His very self to you so that you might be saved. Ah, then you saw how sin could be overthrown, did you not? As soon as your heart understood Christ, then you saw that *"what the law could not do, in that it was weak through the flesh"* (Romans 8:3), Christ was able to accomplish. You understood that the power of sin and Satan under which you had been in bondage, and which you now loathed, could and would be broken and destroyed because Christ had come into the world to overcome it.

Next, do you recollect how you were led to see the bruising of Christ's heel and to stand in wonder and observe what the enmity of the Serpent had worked in Him? Did you not begin to feel the bruised heel yourself? Did not sin torment you? Did not the very thought of it vex you? Did not your own heart become a plague to you? Did not Satan begin to tempt you? Did he not inject blasphemous thoughts into your mind and urge you on to desperate measures? Did he not teach you to doubt the existence of God, the mercy of God, and the possibility of your salvation, and so on? This was his nibbling at your heel. He is up to his old tricks still. As the poem says,

> He worries whom he can't devour,
> With a malicious joy.

Did not your worldly friends begin to annoy you? Did they not give you the cold shoulder because they saw something about you so strange and foreign to their tastes? Did they not impute your conduct to fanaticism, pride, obstinacy, bigotry, and the like? This persecution is the Serpent's seed beginning to discover the woman's seed and to carry on the old war. What did Paul say? *"But as then he that was born after the flesh persecuted him that was born after the Spirit, even so it is now"* (Galatians 4:29). True godliness is an unnatural and strange thing to them, and they cannot do away with it. Though there are no stakes for them to burn us on, nor racks for them to stretch us on, yet the enmity of the human heart toward Christ and His seed is just the same, and it very often shows itself in a *"trial of cruel mockings"* (Hebrews 11:36), which to a tender heart is very hard to bear. Well, this is your heel being bruised in sympathy with the bruising of the heel of the glorious Seed of the woman.

But, beloved, do you know something of the other fact—that we conquer because the Serpent's head is broken in us? Is not the power and dominion of sin broken in you? Do you not feel that you cannot sin because you are born of God? Some sins that were masters of you once do not trouble you now.

I know a man guilty of profane swearing, and from the moment of his conversion, he has never had any difficulty in the matter. I know a man snatched from drunkenness, and the cure by divine grace has been very wonderful and complete. I know people delivered from unclean living, and they at once became chaste and pure, because Christ has dealt the old Dragon such blows that he could not have power over them in that respect.

The chosen seed do sin and mourn it, but they are not slaves to sin; their hearts do not go after it. They have to say sometimes, *"The evil which I would not, that I do"* (Romans 7:19), but they are wretched if they do. With their hearts they consent to the law of God, that it is good. They sigh and cry that they may be helped to obey it, for they are no longer under the slavery of sin. The Serpent's reigning power and dominion is broken in them.

It is broken next in this way, that the guilt of sin is gone. The great power of the Serpent lies in unpardoned sin. He cries, "I have made you guilty. I brought you under the curse."

"No," we say, "we are delivered from the curse and are now blessed, for it is written, *'Blessed is he whose transgression is forgiven, whose sin is covered'* (Psalm 32:1). We are no longer guilty, for who will lay anything to the charge of God's elect? Since Christ has justified, who is he that condemns?" (See Romans 8:33–34.) Here is a swinging blow for the old Dragon's head, from which he will never recover.

Oftentimes the Lord also grants us to know what it is to overcome temptation, and so to break the head of the Fiend. Satan allures us with many baits. He has studied our points well; he knows the weakness of the flesh. But many times, blessed be God, we have completely foiled him to his eternal shame!

The Devil must have felt himself small that day when he tried to overthrow Job, when he dragged him down to a dunghill, robbed him of everything, covered him with sores, and yet could not make him yield. Job conquered when he cried, *"Through he slay me, yet will I trust in him"* (Job 13:15).

A feeble man had vanquished a Devil who could raise the wind, blow down a house, and destroy the family who were feasting in it. Though he is the Devil and is crowned prince of the power of the air, yet the poor bereaved patriarch was one of the woman's seed and won the victory over him through the strength of the inner life.

> Ye sons of God oppose his rage,
> Resist, and he'll be gone:
> Thus did our dearest Lord engage
> And vanquish him alone.

Moreover, dear beloved, we have this hope that the very being of sin in us will be destroyed. The day will come when we will be without spot or wrinkle or any such thing; and we will stand before the throne of God, having suffered no injury whatsoever from the Fall and from all the schemes of Satan, for *"they are without fault before the throne of God"* (Revelation 14:5). What triumph that will be! *"The God of peace shall bruise Satan under your feet shortly"* (Romans 16:20). When He has made you perfect and free from all sin, as He will do, you will have bruised the Serpent's head indeed. The, too, when Satan sees you come up from the grave like one who has been perfumed in a bath of spices, and when he sees you arise in the image of Christ—with the same body that was sown in corruption and weakness, now raised in incorruption and power (1 Corinthians 15:42–43)—then will he feel an infinite chagrin and know that his head is bruised by the woman's seed.

I need to add here that every time any one of us is made useful in saving souls, we repeat the bruising of the Serpent's head. When you go, dear sister, among those poor children and pick them up from the gutters where they are Satan's prey, where he finds the raw material for thieves and criminals, and when through your means, by the grace of God, the little wanderers become children of the living God, then you in your measure bruise the old Serpent's head. I urge you, do not spare him these wounds. When we, by preaching the Gospel, turn sinners from the error of their ways so that they escape from the power of darkness, again we bruise the Serpent's head.

Whenever in any way you are blessed to the aiding of the cause of truth and righteousness in the world, you, too, who were once beneath his loathsome power, and even now sometimes have to suffer from his nibbling at your heel, you tread upon his head. In all deliverances and victories, you overcome and prove the promise true:

> *Thou shalt tread upon the lion and adder: the young lion and the dragon shalt thou trample under feet.*
> *Because he hath set his love upon me, therefore will I deliver him: I will set him on high, because he hath known my name.* (Psalm 91:13–14)

Encouragement

Let us think awhile about the encouragement that our text and the context yield to us, for it seems to me to abound. I want you, beloved, to exercise faith in the promise and be comforted.

The text evidently encouraged Adam very much. I do not think we have attached enough importance to the conduct of Adam after the Lord had spoken to him. Notice the simple but conclusive proof that he gave of his faith. Sometimes an action may be very small and unimportant, and yet as a straw shows which way the wind blows, that small act may display at once, if it is thought over, the whole state of the man's mind.

Adam acted in faith upon what God said, for we read, *"And Adam called his wife's name Eve* [or Life]; *because she was the mother of all living*" (Genesis 3:20). She was not yet a mother at all, but since the life was to come through her by virtue of the promised Seed, Adam showed his full conviction of the truth of the promise.

There stood Adam, fresh from the awesome presence of God. What more could he say? He might have said with the prophet, *"My flesh trembleth for fear of thee"* (Psalm 119:120), but even then he turned around to his fellow culprit as she stood there trembling too, and called her Eve, mother of the life that was yet to be. It was grandly spoken by father Adam; it makes him rise in our esteem. Had he been left to himself, he would have murmured or at least despaired, but no, his faith in the new promise gave him hope. He uttered no deploring word against the condemnation to till with toil the unthankful ground, nor on Eve's part was there a word of lament over the appointed sorrows of motherhood. Each accepted the well-deserved sentence with the silence that denoted the perfection of resignation. Their only words were full of simple faith. There was no child on whom to set their hopes, nor would the true Seed be born for many ages. Yet Eve was to be the mother of all living, and Adam called her so.

Exercise the same kind of faith, my friend, on the far wider revelation that God has given to you, and always extract the utmost comfort from it. Make it a point, whenever you receive a promise from God, to get all you can out of it. If you carry out that rule, it will be wonderful what comfort you will gain. Some go by the principle of getting as little as possible out of God's Word. I believe that such a plan is the proper way with a man's word: always understand it at the minimum, because that is what he means. But God's Word is to be understood at the maximum, for He will do exceedingly abundantly above what you ask or even think (Ephesians 3:20).

Notice by way of further encouragement that we may regard our reception of Christ's righteousness as an installment of the final overthrow of the Devil. *"Unto Adam also and to his wife did the LORD God make coats of skins, and clothed them"* (Genesis 3:21). A very gracious, thoughtful, and instructive deed of divine love! God heard what Adam said to his wife and saw that he was a believer. So He came and gave him the type of the perfect righteousness that is the believer's portion. He covered him with lasting raiment. No more fig leaves, which were a mere mockery, but a close-fitting garment that had been procured through the death of a victim. The Lord brought that and put it on him, and Adam could no more say, "I am naked." How could he? God had clothed him.

Now, beloved, let us take this one item out of the promise that is given us concerning our Lord's conquest over the Devil, and let us rejoice in it. Christ has delivered us from the power of the Serpent, who opened our eyes and told us we were naked. By covering us from head to foot with righteousness that adorns and protects us, He makes us comfortable in heart and beautiful in the sight of God, and we are no longer ashamed.

Next, by way of encouragement in pursuing the Christian life, I would say to young people, expect to be assailed. If you have fallen into trouble through being a Christian, be encouraged by it. Do not at all regret or fear it, but rejoice in that day and leap for joy, for this is the constant token of the covenant. (See Luke 6:22–23.) There is enmity between the Seed of the woman and the seed of the Serpent still. If you did not experience any of it, you might begin to fear that you were on the wrong side. Now that you suffer under the sneer of sarcasm and oppression, rejoice and triumph, for you are now a partaker with the glorious Seed of the woman in the bruising of His heel.

Still further encouragement comes from this: your suffering as a Christian is not brought upon you for your own sake; you are partners with the great Seed of the woman and are allies with Christ. You must not think the Devil cares much about you— the battle is against Christ in you. Why, if you were not in Christ, the Devil would never trouble you. When you were without Christ in the world, you might have sinned as you liked. Your relatives and coworkers would not have been at all grieved with you, and they would rather have joined you in your sin. But now the Serpent's seed hates Christ in you. This truth exalts the sufferings of persecution to a position far above all common afflictions.

I have heard of a woman who was condemned to death during the reign of Mary Tudor. Before her time came to be burned, a child was born to her, and she cried out in her pain. A wicked adversary who stood by said, "How will you bear to die for your religion if you make such a fuss?"

She replied, "Now I suffer in my body as a woman, but then I will not suffer, but Christ in me." Nor were these idle words, for she bore her martyrdom with exemplary patience and rose in her chariot of fire in holy triumph to heaven. If Christ is in you, nothing will dismay you, but you will overcome the world, the flesh, and the Devil by faith.

Last of all, let us always resist the Devil with this belief, that he has received a broken head. I am inclined to think that Luther's way of laughing at the Devil was a very good one, for he is worthy of shame and everlasting contempt. Luther once threw an inkstand at the Devil's head when he was tempting him very sorely. Though the act itself appears absurd enough, yet it was a true taste of what that great reformer was all his life long. The books he wrote were truly a flinging of the inkstand at the head of the Fiend.

That is what we have to do. We are to resist him by all means. Let us do this bravely and tell him to his face that we are not afraid of him. Tell him to recollect his bruised head, which he tries to cover with a crown of pride or with an infidel doctor's hood. We know him and see the deadly wound he bears. His power is gone; he is fighting a lost battle; he is contending against omnipotence. He has set himself against the oath of the Father, against the blood of the incarnate Son, and against the eternal power of the blessed Spirit—all of which are engaged in the defense of the seed of the woman in the day of battle. Therefore, beloved, be steadfast in resisting the Evil One, being strong in faith, giving glory to God.

'Tis by Thy blood, immortal Lamb,
Thine armies tread the tempter down;
'Tis by Thy word and powerful name
They gain the battle and renown.
Rejoice ye heavens; let every star
Shine with new glories round the sky:
Saints, while ye sing the heavenly war,
Raise your Deliverer's name on high.

Five

Satan Departing, Angels Ministering

And when the devil had ended all the temptation,
he departed from him for a season.
—Luke 4:13

Then the devil leaveth him, and, behold,
angels came and ministered unto him.
—Matthew 4:11

Beloved friends, we have so very much to learn from our Lord's temptation. He was tempted in all points, as we are (Hebrews 4:15). If you will study the temptation of Christ, you will not be ignorant of Satan's devices. If you see how He defeated the Enemy, you will learn what weapons to use against your great Adversary. If you see how our Lord conquers throughout the whole battle, you will learn that, as you keep close to Him, you will be *"more than conquerors through him that loved us"* (Romans 8:37).

From our Lord's temptation we learn, especially, to pray, *"Lead us not into temptation"* (Matthew 6:13). Let us never mistake the meaning of that petition. We are to pray that we may not be tempted, for we are poor flesh and blood and are very frail. It is for us to cry to God, *"Lead us not into temptation."*

But we also learn a great deal from the close of our Lord's great threefold trial. We find Him afterward peaceful, ministered unto by angels, and rejoicing. That should teach us to pray, "But if we must be tempted, *'deliver us from evil'* (v. 13)", or, as some render it very correctly, "Deliver us from the Evil One."

First, we pray that we may not be tempted at all. Then, as a supplement to that prayer, we yield the whole matter to divine wisdom and pray, "But if it is necessary for our personal growth in grace, for the development of our graces, and for God's glory that we should be tempted, Lord, deliver us from evil and especially deliver us from the personification of evil, the Evil One!"

With that as an introduction, for a short time let me call on you to notice in our text, first, the Devil leaving the tempted One: *"Then the devil leaveth him."* Second, we will keep to the book of Matthew and notice the angels ministering to the tempted One after the Fallen Angel had left Him. Then, third, we will mark the limitation of the rest that we may expect, the limitation of the time in which Satan will be gone. Luke put it this way: *"When the devil had ended all the temptation, he departed from him for a season."* Some express it, "until an opportune time," when he would again return, and our great Lord and Master would once more be tried by his wicked wiles.

The Devil Leaving

First, we have as the subject for our happy consideration, the Devil leaving the tempted One. When did the Devil depart from our Lord? When he had finished the temptation. It must have been a great relief to our divine Master when Satan left Him.

The very air must have been purer and more fit to be breathed. His soul must have felt a great relief when the Evil Spirit had gone away.

However, we are told he did not go until he had finished all the temptation. So Luke put it: *"When the devil had ended all the temptation, he departed from him for a season."* Satan will not go until he has shot the last arrow from his quiver. Such is his malice that as long as he can tempt, he will tempt. His will desires our total destruction, but his power is not equal to his will. God does not give him power such as he would like to possess. There is always a limit set to his assaults. When Satan has tempted you thoroughly and ended all his temptation, then he will leave you. Since you have not yet undergone all forms of temptation, so you may not expect absolutely and altogether to be left by the Archenemy. You may suffer a long time from his attacks before he will stay his hand, for he will try all that he possibly can to lead you into evil and to destroy the grace that is in you.

Still, he comes to an end with his temptations sooner than he desires. Just as God has said to the mighty sea, *"Hitherto shalt thou come, but no further: and here shall thy proud waves be stayed"* (Job 38:11), so He says to the Devil. When He permitted Satan to try the graces of Job and to prove his sincerity, He let him go just so far, but no further. When he asked for a further stretch of power, still there was a limit. There is always a limit to Satan's power. When he reaches that point, he will be pulled up short because he can do no more.

You are never so much in the hand of Satan that you are out of the hand of God. You are never so tempted, if you are a believer, that there is not a way of escape for you (1 Corinthians 10:13). God permits you to be tried for many reasons that perhaps you could not altogether understand but that His infinite wisdom understands for you. But He will not allow *"the rod of the wicked"* to *"rest upon the lot of the righteous"* (Psalm 125:3). It may fall there, but it will not stay there. The Lord may let you be put into the fire, but the fire will be heated no hotter than you are able to bear. *"When the devil had ended all the temptation, he departed from him."*

Satan did not depart from Christ, however, until he had also failed in every temptation. When the Lord had foiled him at every point, had met every temptation with a text of Holy Scripture, and had proved His own determination to hold fast

His integrity and not let it go, then the Enemy departed. Oh, brothers and sisters, if you can hold out, if you can stand against this and then against that, if you are strong against frowns and strong against flatteries, if you are strong against prosperity and strong against adversity, if you are strong against sly insinuations and strong against open attacks, then the Enemy will depart from you! You will have won the day by God's grace, even as your Master did.

"Well," someone is saying, "I wish that he would depart from me, for I have been sorely troubled by him." To this I say most heartily, "Amen."

Let us think, for a minute or two, about when Satan will depart from the child of God, as he did from the great Son of God. I have no doubt that he will do that when he finds that it is necessary for him to be somewhere else. Satan is not everywhere, and cannot be, for he is not divine. He is not omnipresent. But as someone has said, although he is not present everywhere, it would be hard to say where he is not, for he moves so swiftly and is such an agile spirit that he seems to be here and there and everywhere. Also, where he is not in person, he is represented by that vast host, the legions of fallen spirits, who are under his control.

And even where they are not, he carries out his evil plans by leaving the leaven to work and the evil seeds to grow, when he himself has gone elsewhere.

Quite probably, not many times in one's life is any man called into conflict with Satan himself personally. There are too many of us now for him to give all his time and strength to any one. He has to be somewhere else. Oh, I long to be the means of multiplying the number of God's people by the preaching of the Word, so that the Gospel of the grace of God may fly abroad and bring in myriads, so that the Devil may have more to do and therefore not be able to give so much of his furious attention, as he goes in one direction and then another, to individual children of God.

He also leaves God's people very quickly when he sees that they are sustained by superior grace. He hopes to catch them when grace is at a low ebb. If he can come upon them when faith is very weak, when hope's eyes are dim, when love has grown cold, then he thinks that he will make an easy capture. But where we are filled with the Spirit as the Master was (God grant that we may be), he looks us up and down, and he quickly veers off. Like an old pirate who stays on the lookout for merchant vessels, when he meets with ships that have plenty of guns on board and hardy hands to give him a warm reception, he goes after some other craft not quite so well able to resist his assaults.

Oh, brothers and sisters, do not be mere Christians or only barely Christians with just enough grace to let you see your imperfections. But pray to God to give you mighty grace, so that you may *"be strong in the Lord, and in the power of his might"* (Ephesians 6:10). Then, after the Devil has tested you and found that the Lord is with you and that God dwells in you, you may expect that, as it was with your Master, so it will be with you: Satan will leave you.

Sometimes I think, however, that Satan personally leaves us because he knows that, for some men, not to be tempted is a greater danger than to be tempted. "Oh," you say, "how can that be?" Brothers, sisters, do you know nothing of carnal security, of being left—as you think—to grow in grace and to be very calm, very happy, very useful, and to find beneath you a sea of glass with not a ripple on the surface? You say, "Yes, I do know that experience and have been thankful for it."

But at the same time, have you ever found creeping over you the idea that you are a somebody, that you are becoming wonderfully experienced, that you are an important child of God, rich and increased in goods? Have you ever been like David, who wrote these words: *"In my prosperity I said, I shall never be moved"* (Psalm 30:6)?

Possibly you have looked suspiciously on some of your friends who have been trembling and timid, crying to God from day to day to keep them. You have been Sir Mighty, Lord Great-One, and everybody should bow down before you. Ah, yes, you have now fallen into a worse condition than even those are in who are tempted of Satan! A calm in the tropics is more to be dreaded than a tempest. In such a calm everything becomes still and stagnant. The ship scarcely moves. It is like a painted ship on a painted sea, and it gets to be in something like the state described by Coleridge's *Ancient Mariner*:

> The very deep did rot:
> Alas, that ever this should be!
> And slimy things with legs did crawl
> Over the slimy sea.

"Oh," you say, "that is horrible!" Yes, and that is the tendency of a soul that is at peace with itself and is not *"emptied from vessel to vessel"* (Jeremiah 48:11). I fear that is often the case with those who believe themselves to be supernaturally holy.

A curious fact can be proved by abundant evidence, namely, that the boast of human perfection is closely followed by obscenity and licentiousness. The most unclean sects that have ever defaced the pages of history have been established by those who had the notion that they were beyond temptation, that they had ceased to sin and never could transgress again.

"Ah," says Satan, "this notion does my work a great deal better than tempting a man. When I tempt him, then he stands up to resist me. He has his eyes open; he grasps his sword and puts on his helmet. He cries to God, 'Lord, help me!' as he watches night and day. The more tempted he is, the more he looks to God for strength. But if I leave him quite alone, and he goes to sleep, then he is not in the battle. If he begins to feel quite secure, then I can steal in upon him secretly, and make a speedy end of him." This is one reason that Satan leaves some men untempted. A roaring Devil is better than a sleeping Devil. There is no temptation much worse than that of never being tempted at all.

Again, I do not doubt that Satan leaves us—for I know that he must—when the

Lord says to him what He said in the wilderness, *"Get thee hence, Satan"* (Matthew 4:10). The Lord does say that when He sees one of His poor children dragged about, tortured, wounded, and bleeding. He says, *"'Get thee hence, Satan.'* I permit you to fetch in My stray sheep, but not to worry them to death. *'Get thee hence, Satan.'"* The old Hell-Dog knows his Master, and he flies at once.

This voice of God will come when the Lord sees that we cast ourselves wholly upon Him. In casting our burdens upon the Lord, we might not be able to get rid of them. The better way is to cast both ourselves and our burdens upon the Lord. The best way of all is to get rid of the burdens entirely, to cast ourselves without our burdens upon the Lord.

Let me tell you a story of a gentleman who, riding along in his wagon, saw a man carrying a heavy pack and asked him if he would like a ride. "Yes, and thank you, sir." But the man kept his pack on his back while riding. When the gentleman asked why he did not take his pack off and set it down, the man replied, "Why, sir, it is so kind of you to give me a ride that I do not want to impose on your good nature, so I thought I would carry the pack myself."

"Well," said the other, "you see, it makes no difference to me whether you carry it or do not carry it, for I am carrying you and your pack. You might as well unstrap it and set it down."

In the same way, dear friend, when you cast your burden upon God, unstrap it and set it down. Why should you carry it yourself when God is prepared to bear it? Beloved, there are times when we forget that we can come and absolutely yield ourselves, saying,

> Lord, here I am—tempted, poor, and weak—but I come and rest in You. I do not know what to ask at Your hands, but Your servant has said in Psalm 55:22, *'Cast thy burden upon the LORD, and he shall sustain thee: he shall never suffer the righteous to be moved.'* I lie at Your feet, Lord. Here I am; here would I be. Do with me what seems good in Your sight, only deal in tender mercy with Your servant.

Then will the Lord rebuke the Enemy. The waves of the sea will be still, and there will come a great calm.

So much for the Devil leaving the one who is tempted. He does so—he must do so—when God commands it.

Ministering Angels

Now, let us turn our attention to the angels ministering to the tempted One. The angels came and ministered to our Lord after Satan was gone.

Notice that they did not come while our Lord was in the battle. Why not? Because it was necessary that He should tread the winepress alone (Isaiah 63:3), and because it was more glorious for Him to have no one with Him! Had there been any angels there to help Him in the duel with the Adversary, they might have shared the honor of the victory. But they were stopped until the fight was over. When the Foe was gone, then the angels came.

It has been noted that Scripture does not say that the angels came very often and ministered to Jesus. This makes me think that they were always near, that they hovered within earshot, watching and ready to interpose if they might. They were a bodyguard around our Lord, even as they are today around His people. *"Are they not all ministering spirits, sent forth to minister for them who shall be heirs of salvation?"* (Hebrews 1:14).

The moment that the fight was over, the angels came and ministered to Christ. Why was that? First, I suppose, because as a man He was especially exhausted. We are told that He was hungry, and this shows exhaustion. Besides that, the strain of forty days' temptation must have been immense. Men can bear up under stress, but when it eases, then they fall. Elijah did wonders, smote the priests of Baal, and behaved like a hero. But after it was all over, Elijah failed. As man, our Lord was subject to the sinless infirmities of our flesh. Thus He needed the angels to come and minister to Him, even as the angel did in the garden after the agony and bloody sweat.

It was also because, being man, He was to partake of the ministry that God had al-lotted to man. God has appointed angels to watch over His own people. Inasmuch as Jesus is our Brother, and since all of God's children are partakers of the ministry of angels, Christ Himself also shared in the same ministry. Thus, He showed how He took our weaknesses upon Himself and therefore needed and received the help that the Father has promised to all of His chil-dren.

Also, was it not because He was so be-loved of the angels, and they were so loyal to Him? They must have wondered when they saw Him born on earth and living here in poverty. When they saw Him tempted of the Enemy, they must have loathed the Adversary. How could Satan be permitted to come so near their pure and holy Master?

I think that Milton could have best pictured this scene. He would have described every one of the seraphim as longing to let his sword of flame find a scabbard in the heart of the foul Fiend that dared to come so near to the Prince of purity. But they could not interfere. However, as soon as they were permitted, they joyfully came and ministered to Him.

And does it not also go to show that His was a nature very sensitive to the angelic touch? You and I are hard-hearted and coarse, and thus spiritually dull.

> Myriads of spirits throng the air:
> They are about us now.

Women are to cover their heads in worship *"because of the angels"* (1 Corinthians 11:10). Many acts of decorum in holy worship are to be kept up *"because of the angels."* The angels are innumerable and are sent to minister to us, but we are not aware of them—often we do not perceive them. But Jesus was all tenderness and sensitivity. He knew that the angels were there, so it was easy for them to come and minister to Him. What they did in ministering to Him we cannot tell. I certainly think that they sustained His bodily nature, for he was hungry, and they readily brought food to Him. But they also sustained His mental and His spiritual nature with words of comfort. The sight of them must have reminded Him of His Father's house, reminded Him of the glory that He had laid aside. The sight of them proved that the Father did not forget Him, because He had sent the household troops of heaven to help and support His Son. The sight of them must have made Him anticipate the day of which the poet sang:

They brought His chariot from above,
To bear Him to His throne,
Clapp'd their triumphant wings, and cried,
"The glorious work is done."

Now, beloved, if we are tempted, will we have any angels to help us? Well, we will have the equivalent of angels, certainly. Oftentimes, after a temptation, God sends His human messengers. Many of you can tell how, when you have heard the Word after a bad time of temptation, the gospel message has been wonderfully sweet to you. You have sat in your pew and said,

"God sent that sermon on purpose for me." Or if you have not had a sermon, you have read the Bible, and the words have seemed to burn and glow on the page, warming your soul by their heat.

Has it not been so with you often? Are not all the holy things more sweet after trial than they were before? Have you not found them so? I give my willing witness that never does Christ seem so precious, never do the promises seem so rich and rare, never does evangelical doctrine cling so closely to my heart, and my heart to it, as after a time of painful trial when I have been laid aside from holy service and racked with anguish. Oh, then the angels come and minister to us in the form of men who preach the Word or in the form of the living page of God's written Word!

I have noticed, too, that God sometimes cheers His tempted people with clear sunshine after rain by some very gracious providence. Something happens that they could not have looked for, so pleasant, so altogether helpful, that they have had to burst into singing, though just before they had been sighing. The cage door was set wide open, and God's bird had such a flight. It sang so sweetly as it mounted up to heaven's gate that the soul seemed transformed into a holy lark in its ascending music. Have you not found the Lord very gracious to you after some severe trial or some strong temptation? I believe that this is or will be the testimony of many experienced Christians.

As there come these choice providences, so, I do not doubt, there come actual angels ministering to us, though we are unaware of their presence. They can suggest holy thoughts to bring us comfort. But above the angels, far superior to angelic help, is the Holy Spirit, the Comforter. How sweetly can He bind up every wound and make it even sing as it heals! He makes the bones that God had broken to rejoice (Psalm 51:8) and fills us with a deeper experience of delight than we have ever known before.

Well now, I suppose that some of you are in this same condition. Satan has left you, and angels are ministering to you. If so, you are very happy. Bless God for it. There is a great calm. Thank God for the calm after the storm. I hope, my beloved, that you are the stronger for what you have endured and that the conflict has matured you and prepared you for something better.

Now, what did our Lord do after the Devil had left Him, and the angels had come to minister to Him? Did He go home, stop there, and begin to sing of His delightful experiences? No, we find Him preaching directly afterward, full of the Spirit of God. He went everywhere proclaiming the kingdom. He was found in the synagogue or on the hillside. In the same proportion that the Spirit of God had enabled Him to overcome the Enemy, we find Him going forth to spend that strength in the service of His Father.

Oh, tempted one, have you been granted a respite? Spend that respite for Him who gave it to you. Is it calm now after a storm? Go and sow your fields with the good seed. Have you wiped your eyes, and are your salty tears gone? Go, sing a psalm to your Beloved. Go down to His vineyard, take the foxes, prune the vines, and dig around them. Do necessary work for Him who has done so much for you.

Listen. You have been set free. There are many under bondage to Satan—not free as you are—fighting against him, but still his willing slaves. Oh, come, my brother, God has set you free, so go after them! Go after the fallen woman and the drunken man. Go, seek, and find the most debauched, the most depraved. Especially look after any of your own household who have played the prodigal.

Oh, come, let us go and find them!
In the paths of death they roam:
At the close of the day
'Twill be sweet to say,
"I have brought some lost one home."

And it will be right to say it, if the Lord has
dealt so well with you.

Limitations on Rest

Now, I have to close by reminding you of
the third point, which is a searching truth,
namely, the limitation of our rest.

Satan left Christ *"for a season,"* or,
"until an opportune time." Did the Devil assail our Lord again? I am sure that he personally did; but he did so in many ways by
others also.

I notice that, before long, he tried to
entangle Jesus in His speech. That is a very
easy thing to do with us. Somebody can
take up something that I have said, twist it
from its context, and make it sound and
seem totally different from what was meant
by it. You know how the Herodians, the
Sadducees, and the Pharisees did this with
our Lord. They tried to entrap Jesus with
His words. In all that, Satan urged them
on. Satan also actively opposed Christ's

ministry, and Christ opposed Satan. But Jesus won the day, for He saw Satan fall like lightning from heaven.

A still more artful plan was that by which the Devil's servants, the demons that were cast out of possessed people, called Jesus *"the Son of God"* (Mark 3:11). He rebuked them because He did not want any testimony from them (v. 12). No doubt the Devil thought it a very cunning thing to praise the Savior, because then the Savior's friends would begin to be suspicious of Him, if He was praised by the Devil. This was a deep trick, but the Master made him hold his tongue. You remember how He commanded on one occasion, *"Hold thy peace, and come out of him"* (Mark 1:25). It was something like this, "Quiet, dog! Down, dog! Come out!" Christ was never very polite with Satan. A few words and very strong ones are all that are necessary for this Arch-prince of wickedness.

Satan tempted our Lord through Peter. That is a plan that he has often tried with me, sending a friend of mine to do his dirty work. Peter took his Lord and rebuked Him when He spoke about being spit upon and put to death. Then the Lord said, *"Get thee behind me, Satan"* (Mark 8:33). Jesus could see the Devil using Peter's tenderness to try to divert Him from His self-sacrifice. Oh, how often has Satan tempted us that way, entangling us in our speech, opposing us in our work, praising us out of wicked motives to try to deceive us, and then sending some friend to try to divert us from holy self-denial!

There were also occasions when our hearts sink in our Lord. Thus we read in John 12:27, *"Now is my soul troubled."* He seems to have been very heavy in heart at that time. But the deepest sinking of soul was when, in the garden, He cried, *"My soul is exceeding sorrowful, even unto death"* (Matthew 26:38). Satan had a hand in that vexing trial, for the Lord had said, *"The prince of this world cometh"* (John 14:30). He said to those who came to arrest Him, *"This is your hour, and the power of darkness"* (Luke 22:53). It was a dreadful season. Our Lord's ministry began and ended with a fierce onslaught from Satan. He left Him after the temptation, but only *"for a season."*

Well now, dear friends, if we have peace and quietness right now and are not tempted, do not let us become self-secure. The Devil will come to us again at a fit opportunity. And when will that be? There are a great many opportunities with you and with me. One is when we have nothing to do. You know Dr. Watt's lines:

Satan finds some mischief still,
For idle hands to do.

He will come and attack us when we are alone—I mean, when we are sad and lonely, sitting still and moping by ourselves.

But Satan also finds a very fit occasion when we are in company, especially when it is very mixed company, a company of people who are perhaps superior to ourselves in education and in station, but who do not fear God. We may easily be overawed and led astray by them. Satan will come then.

I have known him frequently to find an occasion against the children of God when we are sick and ill, the old coward! He knows that we would not mind him when we are in good health; but sometimes when we are down in the dumps through sickness and pain, it is then that he begins to tempt us to despair.

So will he do with us when we are very poor. When a man has had a great loss in business, Satan comes down and insinuates, "Is this how God treats His children? God's people are no better off than other people."

Then again, if we are prospering in the world, he turns it the other way and says, *"Doth Job fear God for nought?'* (Job 1:9). You get ahead by your religion." You cannot please the Devil, and you should not want to please him. He can make a temptation for you out of anything.

I am going to say something that will surprise you. One time of great temptation is when we are very spiritual. As for myself, I have never been in such supreme danger as when I have led some holy meeting with sacred fervor and have felt carried away with delight in God. You know that it is easy to be atop the Mount of Transfiguration, and then to meet Satan at the foot, as our Lord did when He came down from that hill.

Another time of temptation is when we have already done wrong. "Now he begins to slip," says Satan. "I saw him trip; now I will get him down completely." Oh, for speedy repentance and an earnest flight to Christ, whenever there has been a grave fault, and also before the grave fault comes so that we may be preserved from falling!

Satan finds a good occasion for tempting us when we have not sinned. After we have been tempted, and we have won the day and stood fast, then he comes and says, "Now, that was well done on your part. You are a splendid saint." You may depend on it that he who thinks of himself as a splendid saint is next door to a shameful sinner. Satan soon gets the advantage over him.

If you are successful in business or successful in holy work, then Satan will tempt you. If you are not successful and have had a bad time, then Satan will tempt you. When you have a heavy load to carry, he will tempt you. When that load is taken off, then he will tempt you worse than ever. He will tempt you when you have obtained some blessing that you have been thinking was such a great boon. For example, in the wilderness, when they cried for meat and insisted that they must have it, God gave them their hearts' desire, but sent leanness into their souls. Just as you have secured the thing that you are seeking, then comes a temptation. To all of this I say, "Watch." Christ said, *"What I say unto you I say unto all, Watch"* (Mark 13:37). In another place He said, *"Watch and pray, that ye enter not into temptation"* (Matthew 26:41). And by the conflict and the victory of your Master, go into the conflict bravely, expecting to conquer by faith in Him, even as He overcame.

But what should I say to those who are the slaves and the friends of Satan? The Lord have mercy on you! If you desire to escape, there is only one way. There is the cross, and Christ hangs upon it. Look to Jesus; He can set you free. He came on purpose to proclaim liberty to the captives. Look and live. Look now, and live now. I implore you, do it for His dear sake.

Epilogue:
Exposition of Luke 4:1–16

*Jesus being full of the Holy Ghost re-
turned from Jordan, and was led by the
Spirit into the wilderness.* (Luke 4:1)

"Full of the Holy Ghost," and then led
"into the wilderness" to be tempted. You
would not expect that. Yet it is a sadder
thing to be led into a wilderness when you
are not filled with the Spirit, and a sadder
thing to be tempted when the Spirit of God
is not resting upon you. The temptation of
our Lord was not one to which He exposed
Himself; He *"was led by the Spirit into the
wilderness."* The Spirit of God may lead us
where we will have to endure trial. If He
does so, we are safe and will come out conquerors even as our Master did.

...being forty days tempted of the devil...
(Luke 4:2)

Six weeks of temptation. We read the
story of the temptation, perhaps, in six
minutes, but it lasted for nearly six weeks,
for *"forty days."*

And in those days he did eat nothing: and when they were ended, he afterward hungered. (Luke 4:2)

It does not appear, therefore, that Jesus was hungry while He was fasting. He was miraculously sustained during that period. After fasting, one looks for deeper spiritual feeling and more holy joy. But the most prominent fact here is that *"he afterward hungered."* Do not think that you have lost the benefit of your devout exercises when you do not at once feel it. Perhaps the very best thing that can happen to you after much prayer is a holy hunger. I do not mean a natural hunger, as it was with our Lord, but a blessed hungering after divine things. *"Blessed are they which do hunger and thirst after righteousness: for they shall be filled"* (Matthew 5:6).

And the devil said unto him, If thou be the Son of God, command this stone that it be made bread. (Luke 4:3)

Satan met the hungry Man and suited the temptation to His present pangs, to His special weakness at that moment: *"If thou be the Son of God, command this stone that it be made bread."* The Devil more than suspected, and I think he was certain, that

Jesus was the Son of God, but he began his temptation with an *"if."* He hissed into the Savior's ear, *"If thou be the Son of God."*

If you, believer, can be led to doubt your sonship and to fear that you are not a son of God, Satan will have begun to win the battle. So he began to storm the royal fort of faith: *"If thou be the Son of God."* Our Lord is the Son of God, but He was then suffering as our Substitute. In that condition, He was a lone and humble man. What if I call Him "a common soldier in the ranks"? Satan invited Him to work a miracle of an improper kind on His own behalf, but Jesus worked no miracle for Himself.

Now, it may be that the Devil is trying some of you right now. You are very poor, or business is going very awkwardly, and Satan suggests that you should help yourself in an improper manner. He tells you that you can get out of your trouble very easily by some action that, although it may not be strictly right, may not be so very wrong after all. He said to Jesus, *"If thou be the Son of God, command this stone that it be made bread."*

> *And Jesus answered him, saying, It is written....* (Luke 4:4)

That is Christ's sword. See how swiftly

He drew it out of its sheath. What a sharp two-edged sword is this to be used against Satan! You also, believer, have this powerful weapon in your hand. Let no man take it from you. Believe in the inspiration of Scripture. Just now there is a fierce attack on the book of Deuteronomy. It is a very curious thing that all the texts Christ used during the temptation were taken out of Deuteronomy, as if that was to be the very armory out of which He would select this true Jerusalem blade, with which He would overcome the Tempter. *"It is written." "It is written."*

> *Man shall not live by bread alone, but by every word of God.*   (Luke 4:4)

"God can sustain me without my turning the stone into bread. God can bring me through my trouble without my saying or doing anything wrong. I am not dependent on the outward and visible." If you can feel like that, if you can appropriate the promise of God and quote it to Satan saying, *"It is written,"* using it as Christ did, you will emerge a conqueror in the time of temptation even as He did.

> *And the devil...*   (Luke 4:5)

He tried Him again. Wave upon wave tried to wash the Son of man off His feet.

...taking him up into an high mountain, showed unto him all the kingdoms of the world in a moment of time. (Luke 4:5)

Skeptics have asked how Satan could have done that. Well, they had better ask the one who did it. He knows more about them, and they know more about him, than I do. He did it, I am sure, for here it is written that he *"showed unto him all the kingdoms of the world in a moment of time."*

And the devil said unto him, All this power will I give thee, and the glory of them: for that is delivered unto me; and to whomsoever I will I give it.
(Luke 4:6)

Does he not talk proudly in the presence of his Lord and Master? What an audacious dog he must have been to howl in the presence of Him who could have destroyed him by a look or a word if He had wished to do so!

If thou therefore wilt worship me, all shall be thine.
And Jesus answered and said unto him, Get thee behind me, Satan. (Luke 4:7–8)

The temptation annoyed Him; it was so foreign to His holy nature. It vexed His gracious spirit, so He cried out indignantly to the Tempter: *"Get thee behind me, Satan."*

For it is written...   (Luke 4:8)

Here flashed forth the sword again.

Thou shalt worship the Lord thy God, and him only shalt thou serve.
(Luke 4:8)

Then let us pay no reverence, no worship, to any but God. Consciences and minds are made for God alone. Before Him let us bow. But if all the world were offered to us for a moment's idolatry, let us not fall into the snare of the Tempter.

And he brought him to Jerusalem....
(Luke 4:9)

Satan now takes Christ to holy ground. Temptations are generally more severe there.

...set him on a pinnacle of the temple...
(Luke 4:9)

The highest point of all—elevated high above the earth.

*...and said unto him, If thou be the Son
of God, cast thyself down from hence:
For it is written, He shall give his angels
charge over thee, to keep thee:
And in their hands they shall bear thee
up, lest at any time thou dash thy foot
against a stone.* (Luke 4:9–11)

At this point Satan tries to quote
Scripture, as he can do when it suits his
purpose, but he never quotes it correctly.
You young believers who go out preaching,
mind that you do not imitate the Devil by
quoting part of a text or quoting Scripture
incorrectly. He did it, however, with a purpose: not by accident or from forgetfulness,
he left out the very necessary words, *"In all
thy ways." "He shall give his angels charge
over thee, to keep thee in all thy ways"*
(Psalm 91:11). Satan left out those last four
words, for it was not the way of a child of
God to jump down from a pinnacle of the
temple headlong into the gulf beneath.

*And Jesus answering said unto him, It
is said, Thou shalt not tempt the Lord
thy God.* (Luke 4:12)

Do nothing presumptuously. Do nothing that would in any way try to lead the
Lord to act otherwise than according to His

settled laws, which are always right and good.

> And when the devil had ended all the temptation, he departed from him for a season.
> And Jesus returned in the power of the Spirit into Galilee. (Luke 4:13–14)

He had not lost anything by the temptation; *"the power of the Spirit"* was still upon him.

> And there went out a fame of him through all the region round about.
> And he taught in their synagogues, being glorified of all. (Luke 4:14–15)

He became popular. The people were drawn to Him and were glad to hear Him. He who has endured secret temptation and private conflict is prepared to bear open success without being elevated by it. Have you stood toe to toe with Satan? You will think little of the applause or of the attacks of your fellowmen.